PERFORMING
HAYDN'S
The Creation

Music: *Scholarship and Performance*
Thomas Binkley, General Editor

Heute Dienstag den 19ten März 1799.

Wird in dem K. K. Hoftheater nächst der Burg
aufgeführt:

Die Schöpfung.

Ein Oratorium

in Musik gesetzt

von Herrn Joseph Haydn, Doktor der Tonkunst, und hochfürstlich = Esterházyschen Kapellmeister.

Nichts kann für Haydn schmeichelhafter seyn, als der Beyfall des Publikums. Den zu verdienen hat er sich stäts eifrigst bestrebt, und ihn bereits oft, und mehr, als er es sich versprechen durfte, zu erwerben das Glück gehabt. Nun hoffet er zwar für das hier angekündigte Werk diejenige Gesinnung, die er zu seinem innigen Troste und Danke bis jetzt erfahren hat, ebenfalls zu finden; doch wünscht er noch, daß auf den Fall, wo zur Aeußerung des Beyfalls sich etwann die Gelegenheit ergäbe, ihm gestattet seyn möge, denselben wohl als ein höchstschätzbares Merkmahl der Zufriedenheit, nicht aber als einen Befehl zur Wiederhohlung irgend eines Stückes anzusehen, weil sonst die genaue Verbindung der einzelnen Theile, aus deren ununterbrochenen Folge die Wirkung des Ganzen entspringen soll, nothwendig zerstöret, und dadurch das Vergnügen, dessen Erwartung ein vielleicht zu günstiger Ruf bey dem Publikum erwecket hat, merklich vermindert werden müßte.

Der Anfang ist um 7 Uhr.

Die Eintrittspreise sind wie gewöhnlich.

Die Worte werden bey der Kassa gratis ausgegeben.

Placard for the First Public Performance of *The Creation*

PERFORMING

HAYDN'S
The Creation

Reconstructing the
Earliest Renditions

A. PETER BROWN

Indiana
University
Press

BLOOMINGTON

Manufactured in the United States of America

Library of Congress Cataloging in Publication Data

Brown, A. Peter.
    Performing Haydn's The creation.

    (Music—scholarship and performance)
    Bibliography: p.
    Includes index.
    1. Haydn, Joseph, 1732–1809. Schöpfung. I. Title.
II. Title: Creation.
MT115.H28B8   1985   783.3'092'4   84-43053
ISBN 0-253-38820-1

1 2 3 4 5   89 88 87 86

For

JOHN F. OHL

connoisseur of choral music

CONTENTS

ILLUSTRATIONS

⟨

MUSICAL EXAMPLES

PREFACE

This monograph arises from my involvement in a projected performing edition of *The Creation* based not on the first edition, but on the materials Haydn used for his own performances. In the fall of 1981 I offered a seminar on Haydn's oratorios, in which several of *The Creation*'s earliest sources were carefully examined. Unfortunately, at that time some of the most important materials were unavailable. During the winter of 1982 while working in Vienna, I was able to study these scores and parts. Some of the results were incorporated into a lecture given in conjunction with a performance of Haydn's masterpiece at Indiana University under the direction of Robert Shaw in November 1983. The present study is an expansion of that presentation.

There is one important aspect of the earliest performances that I do not cover: the problem of the English text. While there can be no question that Haydn intended English-speaking listeners to hear this oratorio in their own language, a series of misunderstandings has resulted in *The Creation*'s text being presented in various "improved" versions of Haydn's and van Swieten's English libretto. Professor Nicholas Temperley has made a complete study of the earliest English librettos (see Temperley/ENGLISH) and has prepared a version faithful to the original English text, which is to be incorporated into the vocal score of the C. F. Peters edition.

My aim is to present material of interest to the scholar and of use to the performer. In the process I hope to have made a small contribution to the understanding of the authentic and early performances of Haydn's best-known and most admired work.

Many people contributed to the present study. Most directly, the members of the oratorio seminar—David Bucknum, Constance Cook Glen, Beth Gutowski, Suzanne LaPlante, Steve Norquist, Robert Schwarz, and Blake Wilson—provided insights and careful evaluations of the *Estate Score,* the *Engraver's Score,* the *First Edition,* and the *Estate Parts*. Ms. Julie Schnepel put the bibliographies in order; Austin Caswell and Mary Sue Morrow aided with the translations. Ms. Morrow also provided some of the documentation for Table 1. My colleagues Austin Caswell and Stanley Ritchie provided expert advice. I am indebted to the staffs of the Gesellschaft der Musikfreunde in Vienna—especially the archivist, Dr. Otto Biba, and Dr. Peter Riethus; the Vienna Stadtbibliothek; and the National Széchényi Library in Budapest, who made my work pleasant and efficient.

The material is presented with a minimal number of musicological encumbrances. In order to save space, however, bibliographic abbreviations are used, all of which can be found on pp. 111–16. Additionally, I refer to performances by the numbers found in Table 1, and to individual pieces by the numbers corresponding to those of the Breitkopf & Härtel Gesamtausgabe. These numbers, with their corresponding first lines of text, are provided in Appendix 1.

PERFORMING
HAYDN'S
The Creation

– 1 –

Sources

WITH THE EXCEPTION of Handel's *Messiah,* perhaps no oratorio has captured the imagination of the musical public as completely as Haydn's *The Creation.* Like the *Messiah, The Creation* has been subjected to more discussion than any other single work by the composer.[1] Yet, whereas Handel's various revisions to accommodate the principal singers have been carefully documented by modern scholars, up to now it has been assumed that *The Creation* as edited by Mandyczewski in the early 1920s, for the old Breitkopf & Härtel collected edition, provides the definitive text. Mandyczewski's edition—whose only source was the first edition published by the composer—has subsequently been the basis for nearly every modern performance.[2] Ironically, it seems that Haydn never used the first edition for any of the performances with which he was directly involved. Indeed, like Handel, Haydn was constantly tinkering with the music, so that we cannot speak of a definitive version.

While Haydn's revisions do not involve rewriting entire numbers as was the case with the *Messiah,* they do provide considerable insight into his own performances. In this study, I will document the most important differences between the earliest and present-day performances of *The Creation,* suggest aesthetic as well as practical reasons for these differences, and assess the true place of the first edition and thus the importance of Mandyczewski's text.

From its first performance on 28 April 1798, until early 1810, *The Creation* was heard in Vienna more than forty times (see Table 1);

TABLE 1 Viennese Performances of *The Creation* to Early 1810

Reference No.	Date	Place	Sponsor/Benefit	Principals	No. of Performers	Literature
1–4	29, 30 April 7, 10 May 1798	Schwarzenberg Palais	Gesellschaft der Associirten	Conductor: Haydn Keyboard: Salieri Soprano: Gherardi Tenor: Rathmayer Bass: Saal	*ca.* 180?	Carpani/HAYDINE, pp. 165–66. Griesinger/NOTIZEN, p. 67. Liechtenstein/CORR, 1 May. NTM, 3 May. Silverstolpe/REPORTS. Zinzendorf/DIARIES, 30 April.
5–6	2, 4 March 1799	Schwarzenberg Palais	Gesellschaft der Associirten	Conductor: Haydn Soprano: Saal Tenor: Rathmayer Bass: Saal	*ca.* 180?	Rosenbaum/DIARIES, 2 March. Sodermanland/DIARIES, 3 March? Zinzendorf/DIARIES, 2 March.
7	19 March 1799	Burgtheater	Haydn?	Conductor: Haydn Keyboard: Weigl Concertmaster: P. Wranitzky Soprano: Saal Tenor: Rathmayer Bass: Saal	180 (AMZ) 181 (Mozart/BRIEFE) 400 (Berwald/ANTECKNINGAR)	AMZ, 20 February, 24 March, 10 April. Berwald/ANTECKNINGAR. Griesinger/CORR, 6 November. Mozart/BRIEFE, 2 March. Richter/EIPELDAUER 1799–1800, No. 6. Rosenbaum/DIARIES, 19 March.
8–9	22, 23 December 1799	Burgtheater	Tonkünstler-Societät	Conductor: Haydn Keyboard: Salieri Concertmaster: P. Wranitzky Soprano: Saal Tenor: Rathmayer Bass: Saal	*ca.* 180–200?	AMZ, 15 January 1800. WZ, 14 December 1799, 22 January 1800. Zinzendorf/DIARIES, 22 December. Pohl/TKS, pp. 66, 96–97.
10	8 March 1800	Royal Palace, Budapest	Birthday of Archduke Palatine, Joseph	Conductor: Haydn	orchestra *ca.* 60 chorus *ca.* 24 (deduced from H-Bn parts)	MH, 1800, p. 370. PZ, 18 March. WZ, 19 March.

	Date	Place	Event	Performers	Forces	Source
11	11 March 1800	Trautmannsdorf	Trautmannsdorf		2 violins, viola, basstl, Flute de Zinck	Zinzendorf/DIARIES, 11 March.
12	4 April 1800	Count Fries	Fries	Conductor: Haydn Soprano: Schönfeld Tenor: Rathmayer Bass: Lobkowitz	9 wind instruments (Zinzendorf)	Zinzendorf/DIARIES, 4 April.
13–14	6, 7 April 1800	Burgtheater	Tonkünstler-Societät	Conductor: Haydn Keyboard: Salieri Concertmaster: P. Wranitzky Soprano: Saal Tenor: Rathmayer Bass: Saal	200 musicians (WZ)	Richter/EIPELDAUER, 1800. wz, 19 April. Zinzendorf/DIARIES, 7 April.
15–16	12, 13 April 1800	Schwarzenberg Palais	Gesellschaft der Associirten	Conductor: Weigl Soprano: Saal Tenor: Rathmayer Bass: Saal	ca. 200?	Griesinger/CORR, 16 April. PZ, 22 April. Zinzendorf/DIARIES, 13 April.
17	6–10 September 1800	Esterházy Palace, Eisenstadt	Visit of Lord Nelson	Conductor: Haydn	ca. 24 instruments 8 singers according to Esterházy pay lists (Landon/C&W V, pp. 63–64) with added instruments	Deutsch/NELSON & HAYDN, p. 115. Jeaffreson/HAMILTON, p. 122.
18	15 November 1800		Orchestra of the Leopoldstadt Theater	Conductor: Haydn? or Müller	ca. 30 instruments (JBTWP), ca. 16 choristers?	Griesinger/CORR, 15 November. wz, 18 November.

Reference No.	Date	Place	Sponsor/Benefit	Principals	No. of Performers	Literature
19–20	22, 23 December 1800	Burgtheater	Tonkünstler-Societät	Conductor: P. Wranitzky Keyboard: Salieri Concertmaster: P. Wranitzky Soprano: Saal Tenor: Rathmayer Bass: Saal	ca. 200?	Pohl/TKS, pp. 66, 96–97.
21	16 January 1801	Grosse Redoutensaal	Wounded Soldiers	Conductor: Haydn Soprano: Saal Tenor: Rathmayer Bass: Saal	200 (Plank/DIARIES)	Griesinger/CORR, 21 January. Plank/DIARIES, 16 January. Rosenbaum/DIARIES, 16 January.
22	25 March 1801	Leopoldstadt Theater	Orchestra of Leopoldstadt Theater	Conductor: Müller?	See 15 November 1800	Müller/DIARIES, 25 March. Rosenbaum/DIARIES, 25 March.
23	4 April 1801	Lobkowitz	Lobkowitz	Conductor: Haydn?		Carpani/HAYDINE, pp. 184–85. Zinzendorf/DIARIES, 4 April. Note: This was the first performance of Carpani's Italian trans.
24	16 November 1801	Schmierer Residence			For a performance of *The Seasons* on 13 May 1803 at Schmierer's Rosenbaum reports: violins doubled, cello, violone, chorus of 16. Conductor at the pianoforte.	Rosenbaum/DIARIES, 16 November.
25	27 December 1801	Grosse Redoutensaal	St. Marx Armen	Conductor: Haydn Soprano: Saal Tenor: Rathmayer ? Bass: Saal	ca. 180–200?	AMZ, 13 January 1802. Griesinger/CORR, 29 December. Rosenbaum/DIARIES, 27 December. WZ, 19 December.

No.	Date	Venue	Occasion	Performers	Number	Sources
26	25 March 1802	Theater an der Wien	Kinderspital	Conductor: Haydn Soprano: Willmann Tenor: ? Bass: Teimer		PZ, 20 April. Seyfried/DIARIES, 25 March. WZ, 17 April.
27	6 June 1802	Pressburg Theater	Birthday of Marie Therese, tenth anniversary of coronation of Emperor Francis			WZ, 12 June.
28	30 September 1802	Augarten	Schuppanzigh			Rosenbaum/DIARIES, 30 September. WZ, 25 September.
29	26 December 1802	Grosse Redoutensaal	St. Marx Burgerspital	Conductor: Haydn	ca. 200?	Rosenbaum/DIARIES, 26 December. Turgenev/CORR. WZ, 18 December.
30	5 April 1803	Burgtheater	Theateramen (Braun)	Conductor: Salieri? Soprano: Saal Tenor: Rathmayer Bass: Saal	ca. 70 instrumentalists, according to WTA 1796.	Rosenbaum/DIARIES, 5 April. WZ, 1 June.
31–32	25, 26 March 1804	Burgtheater	Tonkünstler-Societät	Conductor: P. Wranitzky? Keyboard: Henneberg Concertmaster: Scheidl Soprano: Saal Tenor: Rathmayer Bass: Saal	ca. 200	Pohl/TKS, pp. 67, 96–97.
33	September/October 1804	Eisenstadt, Esterházy Palace		Conductor: Hummel?	See 6–10 September 1800	Haydn/BRIEFE, 28 September.
34–35	7, 8 April 1805	Burgtheater	Tonkünstler-Societät	Conductor: Salieri? Keyboard: Henneberg Concertmaster: Scheidl Soprano: Laucher Tenor: Bevilaqua Bass: Weinmüller	ca. 200	Zinzendorf/DIARIES, 8 April. Pohl/TKS, pp. 67, 95–97.

Reference No.	Date	Place	Sponsor/Benefit	Principals	No. of Performers	Literature
36	24 December 1805	Grosse Redoutensaal	Theateramen (Braun)	Conductor: ? Soprano: Laucher Tenor: Neumann Bass: Weinmüller	See 5 April 1803	Rosenbaum/DIARIES, 24 December.
37	22 March 1807	Burgtheater	Gentlemen Choristers of Leopoldstadt Theater	Conductor: Müller? Soprano: Haser Tenor: Ehlers Bass: Weinmüller	See 15 November 1800	Rosenbaum/DIARIES, 22 March. WTZ, 31 March.
38–39	22, 23 December 1807	Burgtheater	Tonkünstler-Societät	Conductor: Salieri? Keyboard: Henneberg Concertmaster: Scheidl Soprano: Laucher Tenor: Gottdank Bass: Weinmüller	ca. 200	Zinzendorf/DIARIES, 22 December.
40	27 March 1808	Universitätssaal (Aula)	Prince von Trautmannsdorf and the Liebhaber Concerts in honor of Haydn's 76th birthday	Conductor: Salieri Keyboard: Kreutzer Concertmaster: Clement Soprano: Fischer Tenor: Radicchi Bass: Weinmüller	ca. 60 instruments 32 choristers	AMZ, 20 April. Carpani/HAYDINE, pp. 242–46. Collin/HAYDN'S JUBELFEYER. Dies/NACHRICHTEN, pp. 163–67. Griesinger/NOTIZEN, pp. 88–90. Mosel/UEBERSICHT. Prometheus 3 (1808): 15–19. Richter/EIPELDAUER 1808, No. 6. Sontagsblatt, 3 April. WZ, 30 March. Note: Carpani's Italian trans.

	Date	Venue	Society	Performers	Forces	Sources
41	17 April 1808	Burgtheater	Wohlthätigkeits Anstalten	Conductor: Salieri Keyboard: Umlauf Concertmaster: P. Wranitzky Soprano: Fischer Tenor: Radicchi Bass: Weinmüller	Same as 27 March 1808?	WZ, 16 April. Note: Carpani's Italian trans.
42–43	26, 27 March 1809	Burgtheater	Tonkünstler-Societät	Conductor: Salieri? Keyboard: Henneberg Concertmaster: Scheidl Soprano: Fischer Tenor: Radicchi Bass: Weinmüller	ca. 200?	Rosenbaum/DIARIES, 26 March. Zinzendorf/DIARIES, 26 March.
44	15 November 1809			Conductor: Salieri Keyboard: Umlauf Concertmaster: Scheidl Soprano: Fischer Tenor: Radicchi Bass: Weinmüller	Hofkapelle: 35 instrumentalists 18 voices (Köchel/HK)	AMZ, 3 January 1810. Note: Carpani's Italian trans.
45	Lent 1810	Freyinn von Sala		Conductor: Preindl Keyboard: Decret Concertmaster: Ohnmeyer Soprano: Hippi Tenor: Anders Bass: Ignaz Sonnleithner	ca. 60 (Der Sammler)	Der Sammler, 21 April.

outside the imperial city the composer was involved with performances at the Royal Palace in Budapest in March 1800 (no. 10) and in Eisenstadt in September 1800 (no. 17) and autumn 1804 (no. 33). Haydn himself was on the podium for almost half of these renditions and was present at several others. Like no other Haydn work, this oratorio became marked by an authentic performance tradition, preserved not only in contemporary reports from those in attendance but also in the performing parts and scores prepared by Haydn, his own copyist Johann Elssler, and others who worked under their direction. We begin with a survey of the early sources.

First, we will turn to the autograph materials. As is well known, *The Creation* provides us with the most extensive series of sketches for any of Haydn's works. But the nature of these sketches—mostly melodic jottings and brief score attempts—makes their relevance to our interests extremely limited.[3] The autograph score itself is lost. According to Haydn, it was given to the librettist, the Baron Gottfried van Swieten, and not returned to the composer; it apparently disappeared with the entire library of the Baron sometime after 1803.[4] What we do have are a score fragment of the first and second trombone parts for no. 19, the chorus section beginning with "Der Herr ist gross" (mm. 178 to end), and a complete draft for the contrabassoon part (see Plate 1).

The loss of the autograph increases the value of the scores made by copyists associated with Haydn, which often include notations by the composer. Four copyist scores survive, three of which are indisputably authentic; one of these scores was also the basis of the first edition published in early 1800:

> *Tonkünstler Score.* A twelve-line score now in the Wiener Stadtbibliothek (13555 MH), originally from the archives of the *Tonkünstler-Societät* (Plate 2), who often performed *The Creation* at their twice yearly benefit concerts for the widows and orphans of musicians. This was Haydn's conducting score that belongs with the set of parts (*Tonkünstler Parts*) now also in the Stadtbibliothek. Prepared by Haydn's personal copyist, Johann Elssler, and other scribes, it contains—in Haydn's hand—cues for the orchestral parts for which there was not room within the restriction of its twelve-line staffing, as well as other emendations. The libretto is given only in German.

PLATE 1. Draft of the Contrabassoon Part in Haydn's Hand
(A-Wn)

Estate Score. A sixteen-line score from Haydn's library (*HBV* 219, *HNV* 349) purchased by A. E. Müller of Weimar, given to his student Mölk, who then sold it to the Deutsche Staatsbibliothek, and today owned by the library's West Berlin counterpart, the Stiftung Preussischer Kulturbesitz (Plate 3). Prepared by Johann Elssler, the Esterházy copyist Anonymous 63, and unidentified others, it contains numerous corrections by Haydn.[5] The words are in German with an English text added in a hand that is probably van Swieten's.[6] Of all the extant sources, this score contains the most extensive figures for realizing the basso continuo.

PLATE 2. *Tonkünstler Score.* Beginning of No. 28 with
Haydn's Autograph Emendations (A-Wst)

Graz Score. A sixteen-line score in the library of the Akademie für
Musik und darstellende Kunst in Graz, which H. C. R. Landon believes to be "based on, or prepared under the supervision of, the
Elssler copyist group."[7] The musical text derives from a source independent of the first edition and it contains no autograph corrections.
Thus, its status as an authentic source is open to question. Libretto
only in German.

Engraver's Score. The most complete of the surviving scores (Plate
4) is owned by the Gesellschaft der Musikfreunde in Vienna (H
27405). In upright format and copied by Elssler, it served as the

PLATE 3. *Estate Score*. Beginning of No. 5 with Autograph
Emendations by Haydn and Possibly van Swieten (D-brd-B)

engraver's copy for the first edition, which matches it in every way:
page layout, pagination, and an appendix of instrumental parts that
could not be included in its eighteen lines. As in the *Estate Score*,
words are in both German and English. Figures for the basso continuo are given through most of no. 7. Changes in the orchestration
of some passages were written into this source after its completion
(e.g., no. 27) and incorporated into the first edition.

First Edition. The first edition, prepared from the *Engraver's Score*,
was published by the composer, with later issues taken over by Breitkopf & Härtel. The title page read:

PLATE 4. *Engraver's Score* in the Hand of Johann Elssler.
Beginning of No. 1 (A-Wgm)

DIE SCHOEPFUNG ‖ EIN ‖ ORATORIUM ‖ IN MUSIK GESETZT ‖ VON JOSEPH HAYDN ‖ DOCTOR DER TONKUNST, DER KÖN-IGL. SCHWEDISCHEN ACADEMIE DER ‖ MUSIK MITGLIED, UND KAPELLMEISTER IN WIRKLICHEN DIENSTEN ‖ SEINER DURCH-LAUGHT DES HERRN FÜRSTEN VON ESTERHAZY.

THE CREATION ‖ AN ‖ ORATORIO ‖ COMPOSED ‖ BY ‖ JOSEPH HAYDN ‖ DOCTOR OF MUSIK, AND MEMBER OF THE ROYAL SOCIETY OF ‖ MUSIK IN SWEDEN, IN ACTUEL SERVICE OF HIS HIGHNESS ‖ THE PRINCE OF ESTERHAZY.‖ ≫ ≪ ‖ VIENNA ‖ 1800

Containing a subscription list of over four hundred for some 507 copies, it was ready for distribution by 26 February 1800, according to the *Wiener-Zeitung*.[8]

In addition to these scores, four sets of parts survive, and all but one of these are indisputably authentic:

Tonkünstler Parts. A complete orchestral set from the archives of the *Tonkünstler-Societät* in Vienna (Plate 5), copied by the same scribes responsible for the *Tonkünstler Score.* Included are parts for four solo voices (S.A.T.B.); a part for the Direttore (Concertmaster) and eight additional first violin parts; nine second violin parts; six viola parts; eleven parts for cello and bass, including the basso continuo; parts for pairs of woodwinds and horns in three groups—"Erste, Zweyte, and Dritte Harmonie"; a third flute for the "Erste Harmonie" as well as a contrabassoon; first and second clarino parts in duplicate marked "oblig." and "ripieno"; first and second trombone parts in duplicate; a single bass trombone part; "Tympano oblig. solo" and a second "ripieno" timpani part; and ten tenor and ten bass chorus parts. The wind parts distinguish between "solo" and "tutti." A large number of these parts were corrected and changed by Haydn himself. Both this set and the *Tonkünstler Score,* which belongs with them, were unknown to Mandyczewski and were not used in the preparation of the Breitkopf & Härtel *Gesamtausgabe.* Mandyczewski's predecessor as archivist at the Gesellschaft der Musikfreunde, C. F. Pohl, was well aware of their existence; he wrote to Johannes Brahms on 14 October 1876, "One more thing: As I discovered, the Haydn Verein owns orchestra parts to *Die Schöpfung,* written out by Elssler [and] furnished with numerous remarks in Haydn's hand! These [parts] have been in use since 1799. And no one had any idea what a treasure the Verein has."[9]

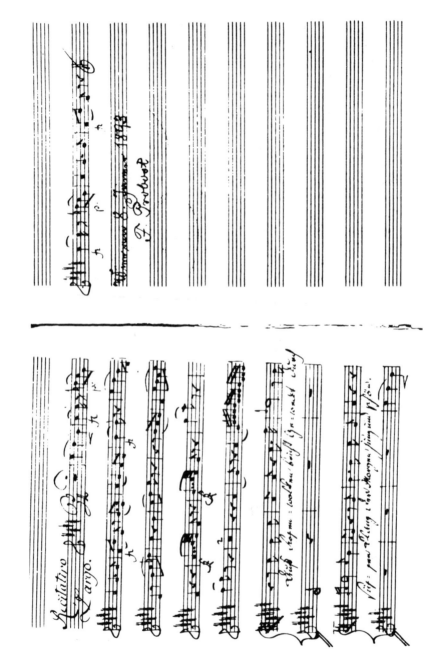

PLATE 5. *Tonkünstler Parts.* Third Flute Part to No. 27 with Haydn's Autograph Emendations (A-Wst)

Estate Parts. A complete set of parts from some of the same hands as the *Tonkünstler Parts* from Haydn's library (*HNV* 350) is now a part of the Esterházy collection (IV 667) of the National Széchényi Library in Budapest (Plate 6). Included are two first violin parts, two seconds, one viola, two cello and bass parts, three flutes, two oboes, two clarinets, a single bassoon containing two parts, a contrabassoon, two clarini, two trombones and bass trombone, timpani, three solo voices (S.T.B.), and, for the chorus: two (one lost?) soprano, three alto, three tenor, and one bass (two lost?). Although containing many small corrections, it is an unusually accurate set that does not seem to have been altered by Haydn.

Elssler Parts. An incomplete set of parts by Elssler in the Gesellschaft der Musikfreunde collected with other sets under shelf mark III/7938 (Plate 7). Extant are single parts for the violins, cello, and third flute. Landon reproduces the now misplaced concertmaster's part in his Haydn biography and asserts that the *Elssler Parts* were the original performance material.[10] Their text, however, postdates in some instances the first edition. These parts may have been the remains from the 1808 performance honoring Haydn at the old University Hall, since the name Kraft (who participated in this rendition), appears on the title page of the cello part, but this performance was in Italian and here the cues are in German.[11]

Sonnleithner Parts. A nearly complete set of parts from the *Nachlass* of the Sonnleithner family, also in the Gesellschaft der Musikfreunde (III/7938).[12] Strings are without *dubletten* and there is no part for the third trombone. While some of the hands may be the same ones as found in the *Tonkünstler* and *Estate Parts,* the watermark is the same as the *Elssler Parts* (three crescents over MA / bow with arrow), but the paper grade is different. It is textually the least valuable set, containing numerous corrected errors (missing bars, wrong notes, etc.). The text mixes both pre- and post-first-edition readings. These parts have no authentic background; they were perhaps used for one of those Viennese performances with which Haydn was associated only marginally or not at all.

One of the central questions to arise concerning the sources is the relationship of the surviving scores to the parts. The *Estate Score* and *Parts* were assigned adjacent numbers in the *Nachlass* catalogue drawn up by the *Schatzmeister* Ignaz Sauer (*HNV* 349, 350). Landon believes

PLATE 6. *Estate Parts* in the Hand of Johann Elssler. First Violin. Beginning of No. 1 (H-Bn)

PLATE 7. *Elssler Parts*. First Violin. Beginning of No. 1 (A-Wgm)

that these are related sources,[13] but the similarities between the two are not convincing. The *Engraver's Score* and *Sonnleithner Parts* contain matching rehearsal letters in red, but this relationship is one that could have occurred any time after 1813, when the *Engraver's Score* and the *Sonnleithner Parts* came together in the collections of the Gesellschaft der Musikfreunde. Again, they are not textually congruent. Therefore, in both "pairs" the connections are merely circumstantial. The only convincing external connection is that between the *Tonkünstler Score* and *Parts*. As C. F. Pohl wrote to Brahms, this material dates back to some of the first performances, and it was used for more than a century by the *Tonkünstler-Societät;* both the score and parts are in the hands of the same group of copyists; both contain Haydn's corrections; and the score and each part are bound in blue with white labels.

Nonetheless, the parts and scores, even those for the *Tonkünstler-Societät,* contain some surprising differences. For example, in the famous depiction of the sunrise (no. 13, mm. 17–19), the lines of the trumpets and horns are interchanged in every set of parts from the reading found in every extant score (see Ex. 4, mm. 17–19). This discrepancy is an important one, for it could not have been so consistently copyist-generated.

The chronological relationship of the above sources cannot be determined. It seems that Haydn did not have scores and parts prepared to accommodate each change or series of revisions; therefore, in order to meet the demand and necessity of performances, desired changes were incorporated into existing scores and parts. Scores were derived from other scores, and parts from parts. In this way, the composer could protect his ownership by having only a few sets of performance parts made before the publication of the first edition. While one could impose a detailed chronology upon the sources based on variances within them, it would be artificial. The only overall valid distinction is between pre- and post-first-edition readings. Nevertheless, one can usefully define stages of composition within a single number.

In summary, there are four sets of early parts, four early manuscript scores, and the first edition. Of these, the *Tonkünstler, Estate,* and *Engraver's Scores,* the first edition, and the *Tonkünstler, Estate,* and *Elssler Parts* have an authentic background beyond dispute. Perhaps the most important source is the *Estate Score.* In fact, it could be considered Haydn's *Handexemplar,* even though it does not contain a large number of autograph emendations. This score has not only the added

English text but also the addition of the Angels' names, carefully made revisions, and the most complete set of bass figures. The transmission of the remaining *Graz Score* and *Sonnleithner Parts* is open to discussion; while their texts are secondary to the above, they present readings that are independent of the first edition. Having provided a cursory evaluation of the sources, we can now turn to the earliest performances and the musical realization of these documents.

– 2 –

Forces, Scoring, and Dynamics

THE NUMBER OF choral and instrumental performers used cannot be entirely settled from contemporary accounts (see Table 1). Reports prior to and after the three March 1799 performances document large but differing forces: *Allgemeine Musikalische Zeitung* (February 1799): "Das Orchester wird aus 180 Personen bestehen";[1] Constanze Mozart (March 1799): "181 Instrumenten";[2] *Allgemeine Musikalische Zeitung* (April 1799): "Der Sänger- und Orchesterchor bestand aus mehr als 180 Personen";[3] Georg Johan Berwald: "The orchestra which together with the chorus consisted of some 400 persons."[4]

At first glance, it appears that the *Allgemeine Musikalische Zeitung* for April 1799 was in error, and that the orchestra consisted of *ca.* 180 members and the chorus of about 220, for a total of "some 400." However, the Berwald number of 400 can be challenged on several fronts: (1) The term "orchestra" often included both soloists, chorus, and orchestra, as can be seen from the two *AMZ* notices: February 1799, "Orchester"; April 1799, "Sänger- und Orchesterchor." In 1810 *Der Sammler* reported a performance where the orchestra consisted of 60 and all were dilettantes except for the first tenor, horns, trumpets, and drums.[5] (2) The *Tonkünstler-Societät,* whose later renditions were reportedly comparable in size to that on 19 March, could not have supported an orchestra of 180 players without using some ninety additional amateurs rather than around two dozen additional players apparently used to augment the membership for the December 1799 performances.[6] Furthermore, a force the size of four hundred performers cannot be documented for any of the society's semiannual oratorio benefits.[7] (3) A ratio of 180 instrumentalists to 220 choristers was not the usual complement; instead, there were normally about two instrumentalists for each member of the chorus in public Viennese oratorio performances.[8] And (4) if we accept Pohl's statement that the *Tonkünstler Parts* were used for some of the first performances, then two players for each string part and one for each wind and timpani part would result in an orchestra around 120 strong. An orchestra of 120 plus—using the rough two to one ratio—*ca.* 60 or as many as 80 singers would confirm Constanze Mozart's and clarify the *Allgemeine Musikalische Zeitung*'s reports, yet completely discredit Berwald's estimate. The total of *ca.* 180 performers for the March 1799 performances is also supported by the figures for other big benefit presentations—*ca.* 200 performers—reported by Beda Plank, who attended the benefit for wounded soldiers in 1801 (no. 21), and by C. F. Pohl in his history of the *Tonkünstler-Societät.*[9]

It is an interesting footnote that after 1810 the performances of Haydn's masterwork continued under the auspices of the *Tonkünstler-Societät,* the various charities, and in the more private environment of the Viennese salons. In 1813 the Gesellschaft der Musikfreunde was established, and oratorio performances took on monstrous dimensions. For the twenty-fifth anniversary in 1837 of the Gesellschaft's founding, *The Creation* was performed in the Spanish Riding School with 1,019 participants (Plate 8).[10]

The renditions using smaller forces ranged from those of true chamber music in private salons to more ambitious public and private presentations. Concerning the smaller renditions, the documentation is less precise and in some cases can only be determined from personnel lists from years other than those of the performances themselves. Returning to Table 1, we can see that none exceed *ca.* ninety-two performers (no. 40), and, not even including the chamber realizations of nos. 11, 12, and 24, some use as few as thirty-two persons (no. 17). It should be noted that the smallest of these performances were directed by the composer (nos. 10, 12, 17, and 18?). However, Haydn's biographer and translator of *The Creation*'s text into Italian, Giuseppe Carpani, would have thought these realizations too small; he gave as a minimum requirement sixty instruments and twenty-four voices.[11]

Regardless of the intrinsic effectiveness of the smaller renditions of *The Creation,* it was not the miniaturized realizations that left a lasting

Einrichtung

des Orchesters des großen Musikfestes zur 25 jährigen Jubelfeier der Gründung der Gesellschaft der Musikfreunde des österreichischen Kaiserstaates am 5. uno 7. November 1837

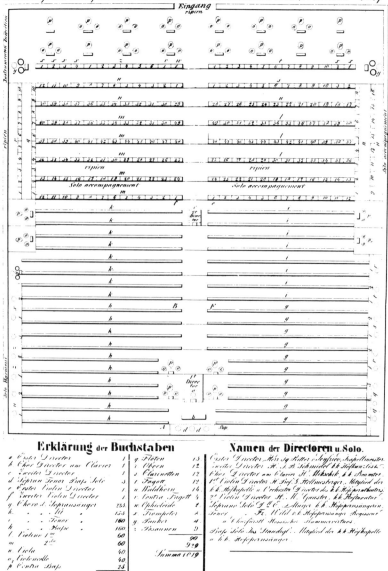

Erklärung der Buchstaben

a	Erster Director	1	q Flöten	13
b	Chor Director am Clavier	1	r Oboen	12
c	Zweiter Director	1	s Clarinetten	12
d	Sopran Tenor Baß Solo	5	t Fagott	12
e	Erster Violin Director	1	u Waldhorn	14
f	Zweiter Violin Director	1	v Contra Fagott	4
g	Chor d. Sopransänger	223	w Ophicleide	4
h	. . . Alt	153	x Trompeter	4
h	. . . Tenor	160	y Pauker	4
h	. . . Baß	160	z Posaunen	9
l	Violine 1te	60		90
m	2te	60		929
n	Viola	40	Summa 1019	
o	Violoncello	40		
p	Contra Baß	25		
		929		
		1019		

Namen der Directoren u. Solo.

Erster Director Herr Ig. Ritter v. Seyfried, kapellmeister
Zweiter Director H. J. B. Schmidel k.k. Hofkanzlist
Chor Director am Clavier H. Mikschik k.k. Beamter
1tr Violin Director H. Prof. J. Hellmesberger, Mitglied der
k.k. Hofkapelle u. Orchester Director des k.k. Hofpernteaters
2r Violin Director H. H. Gaaster, k.k. Hofamateur
Soprano Solo D. & E. Mayer k.k. Hofopernsängerin
Tenor . . Fr. Wild k.k. Hofopernsänger Regisseur
" Churfürstl. Hessisches Kammervirtuos
Baß Solo Ios. Staudigl Mitglied der k.k. Hofkapelle
" k.k. Hofopernsänger

PLATE 8. Seating Plan for the Gesellschaft der Musikfreunde Performance at the Spanish Riding School in 1837 (Denkschrift/25 JÄHRIGEN)

impression, but rather those big ones against which those who had heard them apparently measured all others. For example, A. I. Turgenev, who had heard big renditions in Vienna on 26 December 1802 (no. 29), and also in Moscow, reported on a "miniature" performance in Göttingen and recalled the more impressive effect of the Moscow and presumably Viennese versions.[12] Likewise, the correspondent for the *Allgemeine Musikalische Zeitung* reported that a performance by the *Hofkapelle* in November 1809, which consisted of *ca.* thirty-five instruments and eighteen voices, lacked power, so that the oratorio was not the usual "artistic treat."[13]

As for the sound of the chorus itself, we do know that soprano and alto parts were usually sung by boys at the yearly *Tonkünstler-Societät* Benefits beginning in 1772; only occasionally did mature male altos participate. For *The Creation* performances, however, we have no direct evidence. The choristers were presumably recruited from the various Viennese churches, as had been the case in 1781, when for a performance of his own oratorio, Albrechtsberger recruited a total of twenty-eight boys from the Schottenkirche, the Michaelerkirche, and St. Stephans.[14] The tenors and basses were presumably from the members of the Society, as their vocal parts still survive with the orchestral material while the alto and soprano parts are missing. The first documentation of women participating in the chorus begins after the founding of the Gesellschaft der Musikfreunde. For the 1837 monster performance, Knaben, Mädchen, and Frauen sang the top two vocal parts.[15] If the *Tonkünstler* and *Estate* solo vocal parts are any indication, it seems that the soloists sang along with the chorus; as in the orchestral parts, solo and tutti are very carefully indicated. Thus, the choral color was predominantly male with possible doubling by the female soloists.

In contrast to the extensive range in the size of the choral and orchestral forces, the number of soloists used is consistent and completely documented (see Table 1). There are five characters in *The Creation's* cast: three angels (Uriel, Gabriel, and Raphael) and two mortals (Adam and Eve). Modern performances often use five soloists; Haydn, however, always used three, with the performers for Raphael and Gabriel taking the roles of Adam and Eve in Part III. In fact, the solo parts were not conceived as dramatic characters in the operatic sense, for, as we have noted, their actual names first appear in the *Estate Score*, where they are later additions to the copy. Indeed, not one of the performances from before 1810 uses more than three principals.

Before we can pursue some of the substantial differences between the performance materials and the text of the oratorio as we know it today, one final question needs to be considered: what materials were used for which performances? As discussed, Table 1 reveals two types of presentations: (1) those for large forces (180 performers or more)—the Schwarzenberg, *Tonkünstler-Societät,* soldiers' benefit, St. Marx Armen and Burgerspital, and the Wohlthätigkeits Anstalten; and (2) those for considerably smaller forces (*ca.* 90 or less)—the 1800 Budapest(?), Leopoldstadt Theater, Eisenstadt, Lobkowitz, and the 1808 Haydn homage at the Universitätssaal. The *Tonkünstler Parts,* I believe, were used for every big performance conducted by the composer; it is hard to imagine the preparation of more than one set to accommodate so large an orchestra. On the other hand, the set from Haydn's estate was probably used for some of the less ambitious renditions (Budapest 1800?), as was the fragmentary set of *Elssler Parts* of somewhat later origin. The *Sonnleithner Parts* may very well have been used for performance no. 45, at which Ignaz Sonnleithner sang the bass solos.

Let us look further, then, at the *Tonkünstler Parts.* In this set the winds and drums, as was already reported, were divided into solo and tutti, all of which are carefully marked. The woodwinds and horns were placed into three groups, and one gains the impression that *Harmonie* 1 comprised the solo group, 2 and 3 the tutti. But this, of course, may not have been the case: *Harmonie* 3 may have been verbally instructed to perform only in the choruses and at other climactic points. However, there is no documentation to either support or refute such a hypothesis. While no account of this aspect has come down to us, William Gardiner reports on the balance of the forces for the great Handel festivals held in Westminster Abbey at the end of the eighteenth century, which involved an orchestra of more than a thousand performers. He noted:

> . . . the great softness with which the songs were executed. Although 377 stringed instruments accompanied the single voice, such was the lightness of the effect, that they did not overpower, or incommode it. From the great extent of the surface from which the sounds emanated, they were diffused through the atmosphere, so as to completely fill it. No single instrument was heard, but all were blended together in the softest showers of harmony.[16]

While the ratio of instruments to the solo voice in Vienna did not approach this, the effect must have been somewhat similar. Regardless of what actually took place, solo and tutti distinctions are to 'be found in the most delicate of the arias, and a tutti may occur in the briefest of interludes, as in no. 9, mm. 36–42 (Ex. 1). In modern practice, the

Ex. 1. No. 9, mm. 34–44. Solo/tutti indications

interpretation of this passage is usually not a true solo vs. tutti; instead, the markings are interpreted as indicating to the principal wind players when they are responsible for the leading line.

In the *Tonkünstler, Estate,* and other early parts, there are eight additional passages scored with the bass trombone and/or contrabassoon not found in the appendixes to the *Engraver's Score* and the first edition, or Mandyczewski's edition. In six of these a bass trombone part doubles the contrabassoon, in one the contrabassoon doubles the basses, and in another it doubles the second bassoon:

No. 3—Contrabassoon doubles string bass on tuttis of opening section.
No. 4—Bass trombone and contrabassoon serve as a woodwind bass.
No. 7—Bass trombone doubles contrabassoon in tuttis.
No. 13—Bass trombone doubles contrabassoon in tuttis.
No. 19—Bass trombone doubles contrabassoon also in mm. 149–52.
No. 22—Bass trombone doubles contrabassoon until trio (m. 74).
No. 26—Contrabassoon doubles second bassoon beginning m. 38 (this passage is found in most of the early sources but not in Haydn's autograph.)
No. 28—Bass trombone doubles contrabassoon beginning m. 83.

The complete bass trombone and contrabassoon parts from the *Tonkünstler Set* are given in Appendix 5. Some may think these doublings "out-of-place." However, since the main function of the eighteenth-century trombone—outside of the "subterranean" accompaniments in the opera house—was to double the voices of the alto, tenor, and bass of the choir, the sound must normally have been closer to the bassoon and horn, rather than the brassy sound expected for Berlioz. Haydn was therefore writing for the instrument of his day in a most idiomatic manner.

Viennese trombones could also "blare," and in the recitative no. 21 (Ex. 2) the lion roared more loudly for the big settings than indicated in the first edition; whereas the first edition calls for contrabassoon together with the first and second trombones, the old parts also add bass trombone and all the bassoons—in all, no fewer than a dozen winds, in addition to the strings, imitated the king of beasts. This passage again demonstrates the strong contrasts found in the original parts, as opposed to the less heavily scored first edition.

Ex. 2. No. 21, mm. 6–14. Scoring additions to the lion roar

The independence of the bass trombone from the two tenor trombones and its consistent role as a doubler of the contrabassoon suggests that Haydn originally scored *The Creation* for only a pair of trombones. Such a hypothesis is also supported by the instrumentation of "Chaos" with only two trombones, which comes remarkably close in concept to the wind band interlude of the choral setting of *The Last Seven Words*. With regard to the contrabassoon part, in *The Creation*'s successor, *The Seasons,* the *Tonkünstler-Societät* materials also contain passages not found in the authentic first edition.[17] It is clear that Haydn was constantly adjusting the bass line for effect, strength, and clarity, a preoccupation that dates back to the 1768 letter sent to inform the monks at Stift Zwettl concerning the composer's wishes for their performance of the *Applausus Cantata*.[18]

These adjustments to the parts played by the bass instruments were probably also a result of the larger forces Haydn was conducting for many of the Viennese performances. Perhaps when Haydn attended the Handel festivities in Westminster Abbey in 1791, he noticed the same weakness in the bass that William Gardiner astutely observed: "The loud parts, which it was thought would have been too violent for the ear to sustain, fell far short of that breadth of tone in the bass, which was desired. The foundation was too slight for so vast a superstructure; there was not a sufficient mass of sound in the lower part—nor did it sink deep enough."[19] Thus, by making the sound of the bass stronger and deeper through the scoring of the bass trombone and contrabassoon parts, Haydn may very well have addressed this deficiency.

The exact role of the continuo is left in an ambiguous state by the first edition, which demands only a keyboard realization in the dry recitatives. In contrast, the *Engraver's Score* contains figures from the beginning, which suddenly stop in the midst of no. 7, while the *Estate Score* has figures throughout the first two parts and in the final chorus. It is possible that the *Estate Score* was used by the continuo player for the bigger performances, as he realized the figures at a *fortepiano* supported by both a cello and bass, while the *Tonkünstler Score* was used by the *battutist* or conductor. Unfortunately, the *Tonkünstler* principal cello and bass continuo parts were tampered with, so that it is not possible to reconstruct them completely.[20] It seems that at one point during the nineteenth century the continuo was eliminated and all of the dry recitatives were accompanied by two stands of cellos and one of basses marked "solo"; they merely sustained in the accompanied recitative style what was previously played by the keyboard.

Having established the size and composition of the forces, we can say something about the arrangement of this body for the Burgtheater performance of 19 March 1799 (no. 7). Even though Johan Berwald seems to have greatly overestimated the number of participants, he does provide the only description:

> When we entered, we saw that the stage proper was set up in the form of
> an amphitheatre. Down below at the fortepiano sat *Kapellmeister* Weigl,
> surrounded by the vocal soloists, the chorus, a violoncello, and a double
> bass. At one level higher stood Haydn himself with his conductor's baton.
> Still a level higher on one side were the first violins, led by Paul Wranitzky
> and on the other the second violins, led by his brother Anton Wranitzky. In
> the centre: violas and double basses [*sic* cellos?]. In the wings, more double
> basses; on higher levels the wind instruments, and at the very top: trumpets, kettledrums, and trombones.[21]

From this report, the available descriptions of the setup for Haydn's London concerts,[22] and the disposition of the wind instruments into three wind-bands, it is possible to reconstruct the seating arrangement (fig. 1). The placement of the chorus in front of the orchestra was not uncommon for the time, and without doubt compensated in part for the choral/orchestral proportions.[23]

There has been a strong tendency outside of scholarly circles to regard as a performance practice document the Balthasar Wigand painting executed on a small letter box commemorating the 1808 *Creation* rendition (no. 40) at the University "Aula" (Plate 9).[24] However, it must be remembered that Wigand was commissioned by the Princess Marie Esterházy not to depict accurately how the music was performed, but to record the homage to Haydn. Thus, the scene is arranged to highlight the most important personages present: Beethoven in a respectful stance situated to the left of his mentor, the Princess Esterházy giving Haydn her shawl so that he would not become chilled, Antonio Salieri standing to Haydn's right with his rolled conductor's scroll. In addition, the entire audience is turned to the old master at the rear of the hall—when, in fact, he was situated at the front—and a four-trumpet fanfare normally reserved in Viennese protocol for the nobility honors the common citizen Haydn. Wigand may very well have produced this commemora-

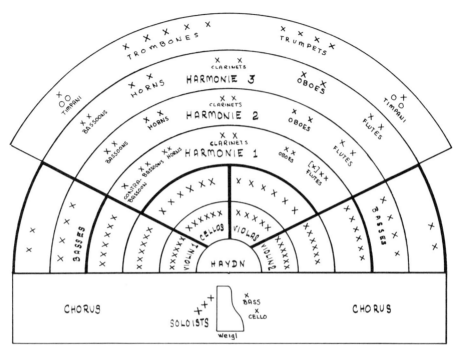

FIG. I. Attempted Reconstruction of the Seating Plan for the Burgtheater Performance on 19 March 1799

tive piece without even being present at the performance, for all the details given in the miniature could have been garnered from the Viennese press reports and the poetic lines written by Heinrich von Collin.[25] That in some cases Wigand's depiction of the participants can be identified speaks for the artist's knowledge of his noble patrons, for whom he produced many similar decorative items.[26] The latter, together with the fact that on this occasion the performing forces were *ca.* ninety strong, which the artist chose to ignore, can only lead one to conclude that Wigand's aim was to document the homage to Haydn and not performance practices.

The Viennese were certainly accustomed to large performing forces being used for the rendition of oratorios, a tradition that went back at least to the beginnings of the *Tonkünstler-Societät*'s semiannual benefit concerts in 1772. What separated *The Creation* from works like Dittersdorf's *L'Esther* (1773) or Haydn's own *Il Ritorno di Tobia* (1775) was its employment of sound—pictorially, symbolically, and dramati-

PLATE 9. Balthasar Wigand's Depiction of the Performance
Honoring Haydn on 27 March 1808 at the University Hall

cally: large numbers of instruments were used to underline what were already unusually strong contrasts, resulting in a total sound with greater distances between loud and soft than any other music ever heard in Vienna. *The Creation* was thus the first work to use carefully controlled and expanded dynamics of the sort later exploited by Beethoven.

Perhaps one indication of explicit control is the mysterious dynamic-staccato markings (see Plate 7) found in the opening measures of the *Elssler Parts*. Landon has speculated that

> It concerns a new experiment on the composer's part to fix the exact middle point of that which is commonly termed, in musician's language, a 'hairpin'—a combination of *crescendo* and *decrescendo* signs such as are found in great abundance throughout 'Chaos'. The original performance material [*sic*—recte *Elssler Parts*] show clearly what Haydn wrote, which was as follows (bars 4–7):
>
>
>
> . . . It was a bold innovation and would have been useful; but Haydn obviously thought it would be misunderstood and so the marking is not included in the first edition.[27]

That these markings were used only in the first several measures of the first and second violin parts and not in the other strings leaves one to question Landon's interpretation: they could just as well represent a kind of *Luftpause* before the beginning of the diminuendo. Without doubt, these marks raise the most vexing interpretive question found in any of the authentic sources.

The most imposing use of dynamics in *The Creation* is the rhetorical gesture that underlines the strike of light (Ex. 3) after the "Representation of Chaos" for the Overture. Here, as is well known, the mode changes from minor to major, the unestablished tonality is suddenly thoroughly stabilized, and the abstract polyphony becomes assertive homophony. The total effect, however, to those at the Schwarzenberg Palais or at the Burgtheater in 1798 and 1799 was much more powerful than what we know from the first edition or Mandyczewski's version of it. The opening unison in the earlier scores and parts did not have the same sound as the beginning to Beethoven's *Egmont*, as is suggested in the first edition, for the trumpets (clarini), timpani, and later the horns were to play "*con sordino*," with only the woodwinds and a pair of trombones left with their sound unadulterated. The muted trumpets in

Ex. 3. No. 2, mm. 23–31. The strike of light

Ex. 4. No. 13, mm. 1–22. The rising of the sun

particular, according to the eighteenth-century theorist Johann Matthe-
son, had an association with "Trauer-Geprängen";[28] the trombone tra-
ditionally carried a related association of "darkness," the "under-
world," etc. When Carpani wrote of the opening of *The Creation* that
"the ear is struck with a dull and indefinite surge of sound,"[29] he was
certainly referring to the color of the opening octaves and what follows
as achieved in the early sources, not in the first edition. Also in the early
sources, the strike of light, of course, called for the removal of all
mutes, and the trombones originally did not participate in this passage;
they were added by Haydn to the *Tonkünstler Parts* sometime after the

Ex. 4 (cont'd)

first performances. The removal of the indication *con sordino* for the trumpets, horns, and drums is first found in the *Engraver's Score* (see Plate 4), where the markings were crossed out before the engraving of the first edition. Thus, the original effect was one of a deeper contrast underlined by rhetorical associations and colors; it is no wonder that some of the first *Creation* performances were interrupted just after this point, while the audience cheered.[30]

The parallel passage of the rising of the sun (Ex. 4) in the accompanied recitative no. 13 is also more impressive in Haydn's performing parts than in the first edition: the species-styled Fuxian texture is now in the major, the climax is again reached without the trombones, and the peak of the line erupts with the addition of the tutti winds in m. 10.

Ex. 4 (*cont'd*)

Although the effect cannot duplicate the first burst of light, it is still without doubt a remarkable gesture.

Unfortunately, the sunset is marked by conflicting texts (Ex. 4, mm. 17–19): the lines for the trumpets and horns are reversed in the scores from the way they appear in the parts, i.e., in the scores the trumpets rather than the horns hold through during the diminuendo both written and implied in the remainder of the orchestra. This particular excerpt might have gotten past Haydn's proofreading, as he is known not to have been very meticulous,[31] but it could not have escaped his finely trained ear for orchestral effect. We are therefore left with an ambiguity: did Haydn mean the dark color of the horns to contribute to the diminuendo depicting the sunset, or did he intend for the bright sound of trumpets to pierce the sonority, underlining the text "In splendor

Ex. 5. No. 1, mm. 11–16, 42–46. Original scoring for trumpets in "Chaos"

bright is rising now, the sun and darts his rays"? In the end, the reading of the parts with the horns sustaining through—which is, of course, what Haydn heard—must be accepted.[32]

There were also other small changes in orchestration and part writing that were made sometime before the publication of the first edition. In the "Representation of Chaos," mm. 13–15 and mm. 43–46, the trumpets originally played what is given in Ex. 5. This passage is found in

Ex. 5 (*cont'd*)

both the *Tonkünstler* and *Estate Parts*, is erased from the *Estate Score*, and not present in the *Engraver's Score* and the first edition. Two authentic readings are also found in the second violin part of no. 4, mm. 27–30 (Ex. 6): the *Tonkünstler Score* and *Parts*, the *Estate Score* and *Parts*, and the *Graz Score* show the continuation of the arpeggiated line throughout the four measures, whereas in the *Elssler* and *Sonnleithner Parts* the passage is changed to parallel the first violin, and the *Engraver's Score* and the first edition follow without correction the first violin. Coming in

Ex. 6. No. 4, mm. 26–30. Original version of second violin part

the midst of one of the most picturesque sections, this revision seems to have been made for reasons other than *Tonmalerei*.

The orchestration in the chorus "The Heavens are Telling" (no. 14) in the *Tonkünstler* and other sources seems to relate back to an earlier tradition of the C-major triumphant affect and instrumentation. In the earliest performances the clarinets were tacet until the Più Allegro (m.

Ex. 7. No. 17, mm. 6–22. The four final compositional
stages

95) and then they doubled the oboes out to the end. The *Estate Score*
added clarinets at the beginning, and it was this reading that is also
found in the *Graz* and *Engraver's Scores,* as well as the first edition.
Within eighteenth-century practice, clarinets participating in a C-major

Ex. 7 (cont'd)

majestic chorus of praise would have diluted the more brilliant sound associated with this characterization. The clarinet entrance in m. 95 in the *Tonkünstler* and other sources shows Haydn's ambivalence in this regard; in his later versions he opted for the fuller, more romantic sound throughout.

More profound differences in the orchestration are found in nos. 17 and 27. As we know it today, no. 17, a recitative (Ex. 7), begins dry but turns to an accompanied texture in m. 6, the beginning of God's words, "Seid fruchtbar alle." At this point the Baron van Swieten suggested in his autograph libretto a "bare accompaniment of the bass moving solemnly in a straight rhythm."[33] From the early sources it can be seen that Haydn followed this suggestion: the Deity's words were underlined by just the cello and bass in the *Tonkünstler Score.* Later, in the *Estate Score,* the keyboard was added—*senza cembalo* is crossed out—and a part for two obbligato cellos was composed, and still later finished with a pair of violas (marked "con sordino" in the *Estate* and *Sonnleithner Parts*). An exercise in the old art of successive composition, this final version, which also appears in the first edition, becomes one of the oratorio's most memorable moments.

The third part of *The Creation* commences with no. 27 (Ex. 8), a depiction of pastoral bliss. Almost as if to draw a parallel with "Chaos," it too begins with a held note, this time a bright E-major

Ex. 8. No. 27, mm. 1-14. The three final compositional stages

chord played *forte* by the strings. In its first version, what followed was a trio for three flutes without accompaniment. Later, a continuo line was written, and finally, the violins were added, playing pizzicato, either doubling or, more likely, replacing the keyboard. Perhaps the original was superior with its finely drawn contrasts of color: string chord–flute trio–flute trio together with strings and horns. Why then did Haydn alter the first version? The answer, I believe, lies in performance problems. In the first version, the entry of the flutes is fraught with problems of establishing a tempo that results in a stable ensemble. The second version, considering the great distance between the continuo group and the *Erste Harmonie* (see fig. 1), would be even more unstable than the first. In the final change, the conductor—in this case Haydn—would be in complete control, with the "metronomic continuo" of the strings within arm's reach of the flutes.

– 3 –

Embellishment and Ornamentation

WHEN CONSIDERING THE subject of embellishment and ornamentation in Haydn's vocal music, one is tempted to view it as belonging to the Italian practice, a style the composer thoroughly absorbed during his period as opera conductor from 1776 to 1790. The Esterházy operatic material seems to indicate that Haydn was conservative compared to what we believe Italian practice to have been.[1] Within Haydn's oratorios, there is a tenor aria from *Il Ritorno di Tobia* firmly entrenched in the Italian practice with its elaborate and probably authentic embellishment as sung by Carl Frieberth under Haydn's baton in 1784.[2] However, it would be mistaken to view *The Creation* as belonging to the Viennese/Italian tradition of *Tobia:* whereas *Tobia* features one gigantic *da capo* aria after another, *The Creation* contains not one *da capo* aria and only three pieces that parallel the more elevated styles of Italian opera (nos. 4, 6, 9, for the soprano).

Fortunately, we have evidence from contemporary accounts as well as the solo vocal parts belonging to the *Tonkünstler* and *Estate* sets to document exactly what Haydn wished—and practiced—with regard to the embellishment at the time of *The Creation*. According to Carpani: "This music requires to be executed with simplicity, exactness, expression, and deportment, but without ornaments."[3] In discussing the March 1808 Universitätssaal performance, Haydn himself told Dies that Demoiselle Fischer "sang her part with the greatest delicacy and so accurately that she did not permit herself the least unsuitable addition," by which, according to Dies, Haydn "meant cadenzas, ornaments,

Ex. 9. No. 7, mm. 73–79, 94–99. Embellishment at repetition of second strophe (m. 94)

Ex. 10. No. 7, mm. 106–13. Embellishment of fermata in all
sources

Eingänge, and so on."[4] Thus, one gains the impression that Haydn
wished for few added embellishments.

The vocal lines in the first edition as well as in the *Tonkünstler* and
Estate Parts reveal only modest additions, which are in accordance with
the above statements. But even within a somewhat limited range of
elaborating the melodic line, one can find a traditional hierarchy, in
that the most extensive embellishments are left to the soprano, then the
tenor, and lastly the bass; that is, the traditional high pitched *seria*
voices are given more variants, and the most extensive embellishments
are found in the soprano parts.

Looking first at the bass, the elaborations in no. 7 are all present in
the *Engraver's Score* and the first edition. Measures 76–77 (Ex. 9) are
embellished for the repetition in mm. 95–96. A second instance in this
same number concerns the parallel fermatas in mm. 91 and 111: the
first is left unadorned, while for the second (Ex. 10) an octave and a

Ex. 11. No. 22, mm. 99–101. Embellishment of fermata in
Estate Parts

half arpeggiated elaboration, which paints the word "Tal" both aurally
and visually, is added. Haydn carefully calculated the role of the ornaments in the structure of this aria, and the singer must perform the piece
exactly as presented in the first edition despite the temptation to em-
bellish. The result as written by Haydn is a slight but effective accumu-
lation of activity in a section of the aria that concentrates on rhythmic
relaxation to portray the calm after the storm of its first part. Else-
where, no. 22 in m. 99 of the *Estate Parts* (Ex. 11) contains a simple
elaboration of the fermata, not included in the *Engraver's Score* or the
first edition.

The embellished passages found in the tenor but not present in the
first edition are all confined to the *Tonkünstler Parts*. It must be remembered that this set was used in performances for at least a century.
Therefore, the ornaments found in the *Tonkünstler Parts* must be
viewed with some caution, for they could have been added at any time
during the nineteenth century. Nevertheless, the embellishments given in
Exs. 12–15, to which should be added a turn on the third quarter of m.
38 in no. 24, while open to question as to their authenticity, are still
viable in the context of accepted eighteenth-century vocal performance

Ex. 12. No. 19, mm. 74–78. Embellishment of m. 75 in
Tonkünstler Parts

practice and Haydn's own preference for modest additions.[5] They could
very well be effectively incorporated into present-day performances.

In the soprano solo, the two fermata elaborations for no. 30, mm.
115 and 218 (Ex. 16), later added in pencil to the *Tonkünstler Parts*,
are reminiscent of the additions to the tenor part. Other changes include
the filling in of the skipping line in no. 5, mm. 29 and 46 (Ex. 17) and a
one-measure *ossia* in no. 26, m. 58 (Ex. 18), as well as the more
extensive changes in nos. 9, 16, and 29. In both nos. 9 and 16 we are
dealing with arias cast in *seria* types; the first is a pastoral siciliana in
the glowing key of B-flat major, while the second is a "bird" aria with
references to the eagle, lark (dove), and—of course—the nightingale.
The pastoral aria (Ex. 19) is already packed with coloratura in the first
edition, which enhances not beginnings and endings but words buried
in the musical phrase: *erhöht* and *Heil*—both of which are especially
appropriate for their respective rising and melismatic lines. Those em-

Ex. 13. No. 24, mm. 33–34, 56–57. Embellishment in mm.
34 and 56 in *Tonkünstler Parts*

Ex. 14. No. 24, mm. 94–103. Embellishment of fermata in
mm. 98–102 in *Tonkünstler Parts*

bellishments not in the first edition essentially have three musical func-
tions: they provide (1) small-dimension activity, (2) greater weight to
the main structural cadences (the establishment of the dominant and
return to the tonic) and (3) localized definition to the brief tonal
meanderings of the central episodic section. Here it should be noticed
that in the *Tonkünstler Parts* only the final cadence is enlarged upon
and with simpler means than in the *Estate Parts*.

Ex. 15. No. 27, mm. 34–37, 47–51. Embellishment of fermatas in mm. 36 and 49 in *Tonkünstler Parts*

Ex. 16. No. 30, mm. 113–16 and mm. 215–20. Embellishment of fermatas in mm. 115 and 218 in *Tonkünstler Parts*

The "bird aria," no. 16, makes use of elaborations in much the same
manner as no. 9 (Ex. 20): turns and trills provide small-dimension
structural action while the elaborations of the fermatas have larger
implications. The first fermatas are the same as in the first edition,
while the ensuing ones are rhythmically intensified as each hold found
in the second section for the nightingale gains in size and activity. Both
arias as found in the *Tonkünstler* and the *Estate Parts* provide models
for the modest use of improvised materials in Haydn's music. Finally,
the performance of the instrumental *Schleifer* in m. 64 and following
is clarified in the *Tonkünstler, Estate,* and *Elssler Parts,* where it is
notated

the first time it occurs.

Ex. 16 (cont'd)

No. 29, written with only continuo support but in the style of an accompanied recitative, is for Adam and Eve. Adam, a bass, sings in a strictly syllabic setting in all sources, while the *Estate Parts* have Eve's section (mm. 27–29 and 37–39) embellished (Ex. 21). These elaborations underline the submissive text and provide a *jubilus* on "Freude" and the concluding words. Such *gorgia* within a recitative by Haydn is seemingly exceptional. Even the theorists are mixed as to whether such writing has a place in an essentially declarative style.[6] Since this is the soprano's last opportunity to sing entirely alone, perhaps these measures were another one of those traditional concessions to the performer.

Ex. 17. No. 5, mm. 26–29 and mm. 45–47. Embellishment of cadences in mm. 29 and 46–47 from *Estate Parts*

Ex. 18. No. 26, mm. 56-59. Cadential embellishment in m.
58 from *Tonkünstler Parts*

Ex. 19. No. 9. Embellishments and ornaments from *Estate* and *Tonkünstler Parts*

Ex. 19 (cont'd)

* EMBELLISHMENT NOT CLEAR

Ex. 20. No. 16. Embellishments and ornaments from *Estate* and *Tonkünstler Parts*.

Ex. 20 (cont'd)

Ex. 20 (*cont'd*)

Ex. 21. No. 29, mm. 23–39. Embellishments from *Estate Parts*

– 4 –

Bowing and Articulation

THOUGH THE PROBLEMS of ornamentation have for unaccountable reasons remained at the forefront of the performer's concerns, a less investigated and perhaps more difficult question surrounds the problems of bowing and articulation. In modern performances, it has become a dictum that all the bows must move together and all the articulation patterns must be uniformly executed, in terms of both simultaneous rendering and parallel passages. However, after one has studied a large number of Viennese scores and parts beginning with the middle of the eighteenth century and continuing into the first decade of the nineteenth, such uniformity of execution was probably an impossibility given the variations, ambiguities, and impressions of the copyists. Was uniformity a sought-after ideal or did articulatory anarchy reign? The answer probably lies somewhere between these two polarities.

It is certain that Haydn took advantage of the effects of particular bowings.[1] On the other hand, even parts prepared by Johann Elssler and his associates and corrected by Haydn himself, as was the case with the *Tonkünstler Parts,* pose many questions; indeed, for the most part, careful editing of the bowings was of little concern to Haydn. I am convinced that the only way to present a performance representative of the earliest ones would be not only to return to the original instruments but also to play from the early parts. If one were to prepare a score that attempted to represent what seemingly took place, it would perhaps require a separate staff for each desk of strings and winds. (Today editors search for a uniform ideal or original text that—if existing orchestral parts are any indication—did not exist in Viennese performing practice.) Yet this reality does not imply that each performer went his own way; the scores and parts provide a general direction, but do not explicate the precise handling of each note or group of notes.

One certainly cannot attempt to solve in terms of twentieth-century practice the many articulatory problems found in the sources for *The Creation,* since these are questions that can only be fully pursued in a *Kritischer Bericht.*[2] However, one can provide some idea of the nature of the sources by turning to several series of bowings from the storm episode of no. 3, an aria for tenor with chorus, as shown in Ex. 22. In the Breitkopf edition Mandyczewski made m. 57 conform to m. 56 and based his reading for mm. 88–92 on the earlier similar passage. Taking into account eighteenth-century practice that a full slur often represents an abbreviation for a more detailed earlier statement, the bowings could be interpreted as follows: the first measure of each series takes a single bow, the following measure, two bows. This interpretation seems preferable in light of the bowing techniques and capabilities of the time and also contributes to the stormy atmosphere that characterizes the passage. The following contrasting measures (beginning m. 97) also pose ambiguities: according to the *Tonkünstler Parts,* the second violin has two bows per measure, and the viola initially plays two eighth notes to the bow. Perhaps the shape of the figure signals four bows to a measure, as does the predominantly quarter-note activity of the other parts. It is very possible that the eighteenth-century string player would have automatically played one stroke for each pair of eighth notes in a figure of this shape. On the other hand, perhaps the becalmed effect and dynamics of the passage are best served by the four-note grouping found in most of the sources.

Although one could write an entire volume on the inconsistencies of bowing in the sources for just this work, there are some guidelines that one might use when dealing with the period in general and this work in particular: (1) The initial articulation for a repeated passage generally establishes the bowing/articulation for the entire group of repetitions, even if a more general marking follows, but it is superseded by a more detailed indication. Thus, I believe, Mandyczewski's interpretation of mm. 56–58 and 88–92 in Ex. 22 needs revision. Articulatory irregularities with regard to large-dimension repetitions in the case of a more generalized articulation are usually parallel, and if the articulation is more detailed, it must be carefully considered. (2) The grouping by

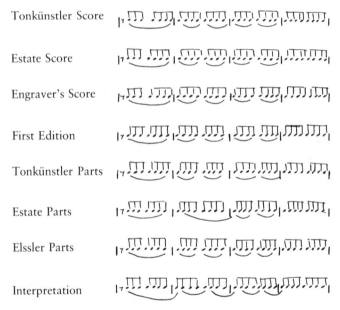

Ex. 22. No. 3, mm. 53–61, 87–98. Bowings in seven sources
with interpretation

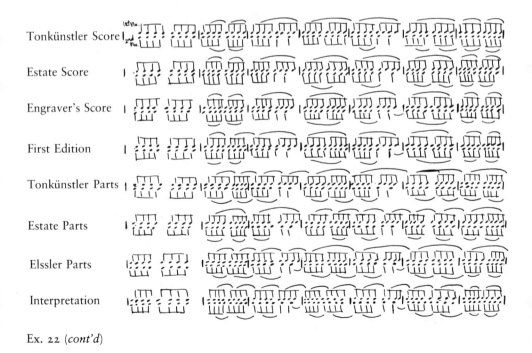

Tonkünstler Score

Estate Score

Engraver's Score

First Edition

Tonkünstler Parts

Estate Parts

Elssler Parts

Interpretation

Ex. 22 (cont'd)

Ex. 22 (*cont'd*)

rhythmic/melodic shapes plays a role in the interpretation of slurs and staccatos (see mm. 94–95). (3) The notation of rhythmic braces with regard to values of eighth, sixteenth, and thirty-second notes affects the articulatory rendition. (4) Specifically with regard to bowing, the consideration of a downbow at a phrase or larger structural downbeat will often help clarify the interpretation of both preceding and following passages. (5) The repetition of the same pitch in values of a quarter note or larger when occurring over a bar line is often meant to be tied. (6) In general, one should not be disturbed by different families of instruments having different articulations (e.g., strings slurred, winds articulated).

More specialized is the question Landon discusses concerning the notation of "measured" as opposed to trilled notation in the timpani part.

The rolls of the timpani, which the Viennese kettledrummers take $\natural$ to mean, are a case in point. As a matter of fact, the Viennese kettledrummers, who have been playing *The Creation* in an unbroken tradition from 1798 to the present day (not a single year has passed in Vienna without a performance), are quite correct. For this assertion we have, most fortunately, autographic evidence in Haydn's own hand. Just before the recapitulation in 'Chaos' (which occurs at bar 40) there is a bar on the dominant with the timpani playing the following notes:

CRESC.

Nowadays this is laboriously performed as sixteen semiquavers—except in Vienna. But in the 'final' sketch of 'Chaos' (Codex 18987, fol 2r., Österreichische Nationalbibliothek) Haydn tells us unmistakably that what he wanted was a long roll. Unfortunately this explanation never reached the first edition, probably because the notation was quite clear to everyone. The sketch is written:

and thus we have first-hand evidence that in slow movements the notation $\natural$ for the drums means, simply, a roll.[3]

The *Tonkünstler Parts*, however, seem not to be particularly clear on this point or the Viennese tradition. The passage in question was clearly played not as a trill but as separate sixteenth notes (Plate 10). Whether this notation was added for the original performances cannot be ascertained, but the question of an unbroken tradition of trills does not

PLATE 10. Timpani Part to No. 1 from the *Tonkünstler Parts*
(A-Wst)

PLATE 11. Timpani Part to No. 28 from the *Tonkünstler Parts* (A-Wst)

withstand the explicit markings found in the *Tonkünstler Parts*. Nevertheless, Landon is probably essentially correct; later in no. 28 Haydn wrote *staccati* over the timpani's thirty-second notes (Plate 11). At the bottom of the same page the notation is unambiguous: sixteenths with *tr* followed by a wavy line. Exactly the same notation is found in the sketch to "Chaos."

The chorus parts contain relatively few articulations. This should not be construed to mean that normally each note is to be well articulated; the "character" of a given passage should determine the weight of the attacks. The lack of slurs in the parts results in little ambiguity with regard to text underlay; the bracing of the stems and the placement of the text itself often provide reasonable indications to the choristers whether one, two, or more notes are to be accommodated to a syllable.

– 5 –

Tempo

HAYDN'S PREFERENCES for tempos were overall on the fast side. As early as 1768 he requested in the famous *Applausus Brief:* "I would ask you to observe strictly the *tempi* of all the arias and recitatives and since the whole text applauds, I would rather have the allegros taken a bit more quickly than usual."[1] When changing the tempos of a movement or an aria, Haydn increased the speed whether it involved chamber, keyboard, or orchestral music. He carried out this practice most often in his revisions of the numerous Italian operas he prepared from *ca.* 1775 to 1790.[2]

As for the post-London period, a preference for a quick tempo is again found in Haydn's corrections to A. E. Müller's keyboard arrangement of *The Seasons:* "N.B. Since because of the quick tempo, the storm in the second part cannot possibly be played as it now stands, my suggestion would be to do it the following way, so that the singers will find the right pitch more easily: *viz.*—you will see my suggestion on the enclosed sheet."[3]

Others described Haydn's tempos for *The Creation* in January 1801. Beda Plank, a monk from Kremsmünster, reported: "I noticed that the tempo, especially in the arias and also by the figures, was rather moderate, and not as quick as we do it."[4] Griesinger, who probably only knew of the oratorio from the composer's own interpretations, remarked concerning this same occasion that Haydn "conducted with youthful fire. . . ."[5]

The tempo markings of *The Creation* seem to have been well set in

Haydn's mind, for all the sources present an unusual uniformity. The only differences are as follows:

No.5   Moderato C—*Tonkünstler Score, Estate* and *Elssler Parts*
        Moderato ¢—*Tonkünstler Parts*
        Allegro moderato C—*Estate* ("Allegro" added by Haydn) and *Graz Scores*
        Allegro C—*Engraver's Score, First Edition, Sonnleithner Parts*

No. 7   Allegro assai C—*Tonkünstler, Estate, Graz,* and *Engraver's Scores, First Edition, Estate,* and *Sonnleithner Parts*
        Allegro assai ¢—*Tonkünstler* and *Elssler Parts*

No. 22 Maestoso $\frac{3}{4}$—*Tonkünstler, Graz,* and *Engraver's Scores, First Edition, Tonkünstler, Estate, Elssler,* and *Sonnleithner Parts*
        Allegro maestoso $\frac{3}{4}$—*Estate Score* ("Allegro" added by Haydn?)

In no. 5 the *alla breve* may well be a copyist's error; the ability to control the performing forces would be greatly diminished if this piece were conducted with two beats per measure. The Allegro C tempo is to be preferred rather than the moderato for this chorus of praise; or, to paraphrase Haydn, "the whole text applauds, so the tempo should be a quick one." Though no. 7 is less difficult to control in *alla breve* than no. 5, much the same rationale can be used in favoring Allegro assai C. Haydn's failure to incorporate the Allegro of the *Estate Score* in any of the other sources for no. 22 may have been a move to prevent too rapid a tempo, which would have destroyed any of its lofty associations.

The only present-day performance tempo that needs reconsideration is that of the instrumental introduction, "The Representation of Chaos." In every early available source the tempo and meter are uniformly Largo ¢; nearly every modern performance uses an extremely slow tempo, in which the beat approaches or is the eighth note. If such a tempo is correct, "Chaos" becomes the slowest of Haydn's more than two dozen Largos in *alla breve*. But is so deliberate a tempo appropriate? Stylistically, the movement combines Fuxian counterpoint with the fantasia bass line and unmeasured rhythms of C. P. E. Bach, as elucidated in the *Versuch*. Essentially, "Chaos" is an instrumental movement in a bizarre motet style, a ricercar functioning as an *exordium*. The unmeasured rhythms from the fantasia do not bear on its tempo (i.e., the figures in mm. 31, 39, 49). Thus, its primary unit of movement should be the half or a moving quarter note. Perhaps its closest neighbors are the second movement of the Quartet Op. 74/3 and the introduction to Symphony 102.

– 6 –

Conclusion

WHILE IT IS IMPOSSIBLE to establish with certainty an *Urtext* for Haydn's *The Creation,* which is probably embedded in the *Tonkünstler* and *Estate* materials, there is little reason to doubt that, chronologically speaking, the *Engraver's Score* and the first edition represent an end version. However, neither the *Engraver's Score* nor the first edition provides a definitive text for the way Haydn actually performed the music as revealed by the earlier sources. If this be the case, then what was the purpose of the first edition as published by the composer? The evidence suggests that Haydn's primary objective was to secure for himself a substantial financial return. The edition had all the trappings of a souvenir of already legendary music from the hands of the most revered musical personality of his day, with its prestigious subscription list, special paper, and title page signed and sealed by Haydn himself; for the royalty, the nobility, and the gentry, it was a significant acquisition for their collections.

If performance were the primary objective of the first edition, Haydn would have issued parts. However, parts would probably not have been of interest to many of the persons on *The Creation*'s subscription list. That financial return was the primary object is also supported by the fact that in 1801 Haydn thought it better to print a Mass in parts rather than in score so that it could be performed more readily.[1]

Haydn's own priorities are indicated in the announcement for the edition that appeared in June 1799: "The work is to appear in full score, so that on the one hand, the public may have the work in its entirety, and so that the connoisseur may see it *in toto* and thus better judge it; while on the other, it will be easier to prepare the parts, should one wish to perform it anywhere."² Thus, the first edition was first for the public and for the connoisseur and second for the performer, who must have the parts prepared in order to realize a performance.

Furthermore, if Haydn were really concerned with publishing a definitive performing version, why were the figures omitted from the bass line for all of the main numbers of the oratorio? Why were the solo/tutti markings so haphazardly entered in the first edition? Why were there a number of other omissions and errors in this print? And finally, if the first edition is the definitive text, why is the contrast between the *Tonkünstler* materials and the *Engraver's Score* so striking? The former have many corrections in Haydn's hand, while the latter, though written by Elssler, has no confirmable entries by the composer. Though one cannot answer these questions, they raise not only the issue of intent but, more importantly, one of the care with which the first edition was prepared.

One might also conclude that, like any fine composer, Haydn may have purposely held certain effects in reserve for his own renditions. This hypothesis is supported by the history of the two earliest performances in England, in March and April 1800. Johann Peter Salomon, from whom Haydn had obtained the original English libretto and to whom the composer had contractual obligations regarding *The Creation*,³ received his dozen copies of the first edition on 23 March 1800 only to learn that one John Ashley was ready to mount the first presentation with some 150 performers later that week. Salomon's performance did not materialize until some four weeks later. In the meantime, on 27 March he published the following notice:

> Mr. Salomon having received from Dr. Haydn a correct Copy of his New Oratorio, called *The Creation of the World,* and having been favoured by him, exclusively, with particular Directions on the Style and Manner in which it must be executed, in order to produce the Effects required by the Author, begs to acquaint the Nobility and Gentry, that he intends to perform it on Monday, the 21st of April next, at the King's Theatre, Haymarket. The Names of Performers and other particulars will be advertised in a few days.⁴

Ashley's reply was first printed on 31 March in the expected fashion:

> Mr. Salomon having insinuated that he alone is in possession of a Correct Score of the celebrated Oratorio, I feel compelled in justice to myself, to state, that the Oratorio was published by Subscription at Vienna, and that the printed Copy from which I had the Parts transcribed, was delivered by Dr. Haydn to a Subscriber in Vienna, and brought from thence expressly for me, and on which is the Doctor's initials. The accuracy with which it was performed, and the enthusiasm with which it was received, are, I hope, convincing proofs that no other directions are necessary to 'produce the effect required by the Author'.
>
> I should not have thus obtruded myself, but I conceive it requisite to justify myself from the imputation of having attempted to impose a spurious production upon that Public to whom I am under so many obligations.[5]

Salomon rejoined on 4 April:

> In reply to Mr. Ashley's Advertisements, Mr. Salomon thinks it incumbent upon him to state to the Public, that when he announced his intention of performing this celebrated Oratorio on the 21st of April at the King's Theatre, he did not assert to be alone in possession of a correct score of this excellent Work, but said, what he can prove by Dr. Haydn's letters, that he had been favoured, exclusively, by Dr. Haydn with particular directions on the stile and manner in which it ought to be executed, to produce the effects required by the Author.[6]

Salomon certainly suggests that Haydn wrote him a letter detailing the correct and most effective way of performing *The Creation;* in other words, Salomon had received a letter not unlike the *Applausus Brief* of 1768. Most unfortunately, Salomon's document has not survived and is not known to have been seen by others, but it does seem likely that Haydn may have written such a letter and that it contained some of the readings discussed above.

For the performer, the first edition presents a single reading; in contrast, the materials surveyed here offer a number of choices. Although these options cannot in many cases be proven to be absolutely authentic, they do occur in materials used by the composer and from which a performance tradition came into being. For the historian, some of the variants in the early scores and parts present a continuity that is part of an evolution that can be traced back to the surviving sketches and underline *The Creation*'s marvelous synthesis of baroque textures and rhetoric, classic simplicity, and romantic color. This collocation can be fully realized only by restoring some of the proportions and readings of the earliest performances, which in turn would recapture more of the manner in which Haydn rendered his most popular and profitable work.

Appendix 1

CONTENTS OF THE NUMBERS

PART 1

No.

1. **Overture.** Die Vorstellung des Chaos—The Representation of Chaos.

2. **Recit. and Chorus.** Recit. (Raphael.) Im Anfange schuf Gott Himmel und Erde—In the beginning God created the heaven and the earth. Chorus. Und der Geist Gottes schwebte auf der Fläche der Wasser—And the spirit of God moved among the face of the waters.

3. **Aria and Chorus.** Aria. (Uriel.) Nun schwanden vor dem heiligen Strahle—Now vanish before the holy beams. Chorus. Verzweiflung, Wut und Schrecken—Despairing, cursing rage.

4. **Recit.** (Raphael.) Und Gott machte das Firmament—And God made the firmament.

5. **Solo with Chorus.** (Gabriel.) Mit Staunen sieht das Wunderwerk—The marvelous work beholds amazed.

6. **Recit.** (Raphael.) Und Gott sprach: Es sammle sich das Wasser—And God said: Let the waters be gathered together.

7. **Aria.** Rollend in schäumenden Wellen—Rolling in foaming billows.

8. **Recit.** (Gabriel.) Und Gott sprach: Es bringe die Erde Gras hervor—And God said: Let the earth bring forth grass.

9. **Aria.** Nun beut die Flur das frische Grün—With verdure clad the fields appear.

10. **Recit.** (Uriel.) Und die himmlischen Heerscharen—And heavenly host proclaimed.

11. **Chorus.** Stimmt an die Saiten—Awake the harp.

12. **Recit.** (Uriel.) Und Gott sprach: Es sei'n Lichter an der Feste des Himmels—And God said: Let there be lights in the firmament of heaven.

13. **Recit.** In vollem Glanze steiget jetzt die Sonne strahlend auf—In splendor bright the sun is rising now.

14. **Trio and Chorus.** Die Himmel erzählen die Ehre Gottes—The heavens are telling the glory of God.

PART 2

15. **Recit.** (Gabriel.) Und Gott sprach: Es bringe das Wasser—And God said: Let the waters bring forth.
16. **Aria.** Auf starkem Fittige schwinget—On mighty pens uplifted soars.
17. **Recit.** (Raphael.) Und Gott schuf grosse Walfische—And God created great whales.
18. **Recit.** (Raphael.) Und die Engel rührten ihr' unsterblichen Harfen—And the angels struck their immortal harps.
19. **Trio and Chorus.** In holder Anmut stehn—Most beautiful appear.
20. **Recit.** (Raphael.) Und Gott sprach: Es bringe die Erde—And God said: Let the earth bring forth.
21. **Recit.** Gliech öffnet sich der Erde Schoss—Straight opening her fertile womb.
22. **Aria.** Nun scheint in vollem Glanze—Now heav'n in all her glory shone.
23. **Recit.** (Uriel.) Und Gott schuf den Menschen—And God created man.
24. **Aria.** Mit Würd' und Hoheit angetan—In native worth and honour clad.
25. **Recit.** (Raphael). Und Gott sah jedes Ding—And God saw everything.
26. **Chorus and Trio.** Vollendet ist das grosse Werk—Achieved is the glorious work.

PART 3

27. **Recit.** (Uriel.) Aus Rosenwolken bricht—In rosy mantle appears.
28. **Duet with Chorus.** (Eve and Adam.) Von deiner Güt', o Herr—By thee with bliss, o bounteous Lord.
29. **Recit.** (Adam.) Nun ist die erste Pflicht erfüllt—Our duty we performed now.
30. **Duet.** (Adam and Eve.) Holde Gattin, dir zur Seite—Graceful consort, at thy side.
31. **Recit.** (Uriel.) O glücklich Paar—O happy pair.
32. **Chorus.** Singt dem Herren alle Stimmen—Sing the Lord ye voices all.

Appendix 2

COMPARISON OF SOURCES FOR
IMPORTANT VARIANTS

	Tonkünstler Score	Estate Score	Graz Score	Engraver's Score	First Edition	Breitkopf Ed. Mandyczewski	Tonkünstler Parts	Estate Parts	Elssler Parts	Sonnleithner Parts
No. 1 con sordino in trumpets, horns, and timpani	No, but only horn part included	Yes	Yes	Yes, then crossed out	No	No	Yes	Yes	—	Yes
trumpet notes in mm. 13–15, 43–46	—	Yes, then erased	Yes	No	No	No	Yes	Yes	—	Yes, then crossed out
No. 2 scoring of trombones to mm. 28–31	—	—	—	Yes, in appendix	Yes, in appendix	Yes	Added by Haydn	Yes	—	Yes
No. 3 added scoring of contrabassoon and bass trombone	—	—	—	No	No	No	Yes	Yes	—	Yes, for contrabassoon
No. 4 added scoring of contrabassoon and bass trombone	—	—	—	No	No	No	Yes	Yes	—	—
arpeggiated or stepwise 2nd violin in mm. 28 & 30	Arpeg.	Arpeg.	Arpeg.	Step	Step	Step	Arpeg.	Arpeg.	Arpeg. crossed out, step substituted	Arpeg. crossed out, step substituted

No. 7 bass trombone doubles contra-bassoon	No. 13 exchange of horn and trumpet parts, mm. 17–19	bass trombone doubles contra-bassoon	No. 14 clarinet tacet to Più Allegro	No. 16 notation of Schleifer m. 64	No. 17 scoring beginning in m. 6	No. 19 bass trombone double contra-bassoon
—	horns hold	—	Yes	[music notation]	1st & 2nd viola, 1st & 2nd cello, bass	—
—	—	—	—	[music notation]	bass line only?	—
Yes	horns hold	Yes	Yes	[music notation]	1st & 2nd viola, 1st & 2nd cello, bass	Yes
Yes	horns hold	Yes	Yes	[music notation]	1st & 2nd viola, 1st & 2nd cello in later hand, bass	Yes
No	trumpets hold	No	No	[music notation]	1st & 2nd viola, 1st & 2nd cello, bass	No
No	trumpets hold	No	No	[music notation]	1st & 2nd viola, 1st & 2nd cello, bass	No
No	trumpets hold	No	No	[music notation]	1st & 2nd viola, 1st & 2nd cello, bass	No
—	trumpets hold	No	—	[music notation]	1st & 2nd cello & continuo	—
—	trumpets hold	—	"col oboe" added	[music notation]	1st & 2nd cello & continuo; "senza cembalo" crossed out	—

	Tonkünstler Score	Estate Score	Graz Score	Engraver's Score	First Edition	Breitkopf Ed. Mandyczewski	Tonkünstler Parts	Estate Parts	Elssler Parts	Sonnleithner Parts
No. 21 wind scoring of "roar" notes, mm. 8–10	bassoons & contrabassoon, no staves for trombones	bassoons & contrabassoon	bassoons & contrabassoon	trombone 1 & 2, contrabassoon	trombone 1 & 2, contrabassoon	trombone 1 & 2, contrabassoon	trombones 1, 2 & 3, bassoon 1 & 2, contrabassoon	trombones 1, 2 & 3, bassoon 1 & 2, contrabassoon	—	trombones 1 & 2, bassoon 1 & 2, contrabassoon
No. 22 bass trombone doubles contrabassoon	—	—	—	No	No	No	Yes	Yes	—	—
No. 24 mm. 37–38 C♮→C#	Yes	Yes	Yes	Yes	Yes	No	Yes	Yes	Yes	Yes
No. 26 mm. 38 ff. contrabassoon doubles 2nd bassoon	—	Yes	Yes	"contra-fagotto col IIdo" crossed out	No	No	Yes	Yes	—	Yes
No. 27 scoring of beginning	flute trio, bass added	flute trio, 1st & 2nd violin & bass added?	flute trio only	flute trio, 1st & 2nd violin and bass added	flute trio, 1st & 2nd violin and bass	flute trio, 1st & 2nd violin and bass	1st & 2nd violin added by Haydn	1st & 2nd violin added	[flute trio], 1st violin and bass, 2nd violin added	flute trio, 1st violin and bass, 2nd violin rests

No. 28 mm. 81 ff. bass trombone doubles contrabassoon	No	—	—	No	No	No	Yes	Yes	—	—
figured bass recitatives excluded	No	Yes, but in Part III only No. 32	No	Yes, to middle of No. 7	No	No	—	—	—	—
names of angels	No	Added	Added	Yes	Yes	Yes	Yes	No	—	—

Appendix 3
SOLO/TUTTI INDICATIONS IN
Tonkünstler Parts

N.B. Unless otherwise stated, solo markings apply to entire *Erste Harmonie*, obbligati clarini, and timpani. Where appropriate, the solo or tutti should begin with the pick-up(s) into the measure. The indication of solo or tutti remains in effect until changed. Bracketed markings are editorial suggestions. (See also pp. 24–26.)

No. 1

m. 6 bassoon solo
m. 7 tutti bassoons
m. 13 bassoon solo
[m. 14 tutti bassoons]
mm. 21-24 bassoon solo
[m. 25 second half, tutti bassoons]
m. 33 solo
m. 40 tutti
m. 41 bassoon solo
[m. 42 tutti bassoons]
m. 49 bassoon solo on third quarter
m. 51 all wind entries solo

The solo/tutti markings for No. 1, "Chaos," are not as clear as in the following numbers. It may be that solo and tutti were used here in the more modern sense and that the entire introduction was played only by the *Erste Harmonie*, obbligati clarini, and timpani; the second and third wind bands were perhaps held in reserve until m. 28 of No. 2.

No. 2

m. 7 solo clarinet
m. 28 tutti

No. 3

m. 1 solo
m. 10 tutti
m. 17 solo
[m. 29 tutti]
m. 34 solo
[m. 51 tutti]
m. 57 solo
m. 77 tutti
m. 97 solo
m. 121 tutti
m. 128 solo
m. 144 tutti

No. 4

m. 7 tutti
m. 28 solo
m. 35 tutti

No. 5

mm. 1–4 oboe solo, others tutti
m. 6 oboe tutti
m. 12 oboe solo
m. 16 tutti
m. 30 oboe solo
m. 34 tutti
m. 39 oboe solo, others tutti
m. 41 oboe tutti

No. 7

m. 1 tutti
m. 22 solo
m. 27 tutti
m. 29 solo
m. 45 tutti
m. 50 solo
m. 73 solo

No. 9

m. 1 solo
m. 36 tutti
m. 43 solo
m. 50 tutti
m. 52 solo
m. 87 tutti

No. 11

tutti throughout

No. 13

m. 1 solo
m. 10 tutti

No. 14

m. 1 tutti
m. 19 solo
m. 38 tutti
m. 53 oboes and clarinets solo
m. 54 horns solo
m. 55 flutes and bassoons solo
m. 73 trumpets and timpani solo
m. 88 tutti

No. 16

m. 1 tutti
m. 9 solo
m. 14 tutti
[m. 18 solo beginning second quarter]
m. 19 solo

m. 23 tutti
m. 52 solo
m. 80 tutti
m. 86 solo
m. 115 tutti
m. 120 solo
m. 199 tutti

No. 19

m. 8 tutti
m. 42 solo
[m. 49 tutti?]
m. 53 solo
m. 85 tutti
m. 99 solo
m. 112 tutti
m. 128 [solo?]
m. 133 tutti except for flute solo [?]
[m. 141 tutti?]
m. 145 tutti
m. 168 solo
m. 171 tutti
m. 186 solo
m. 189 tutti

No. 21

m. 1 tutti
m. 40 solo

No. 22

m. 1 tutti
m. 11 solo
m. 15 tutti
m. 18 solo
m. 21 tutti
m. 59 solo
m. 63 tutti
m. 66 solo
m. 82 tutti
m. 88 solo
m. 96 tutti

No. 24

m. 2 solo
m. 8 tutti
m. 11 oboes and bassoons solo
   on second quarter
m. 12 solo
m. 23 tutti
m. 33 solo
m. 40 tutti
m. 44 solo
m. 51 tutti
m. 57 solo

No. 26

m. 1 tutti
m. 38 solo
m. 132 tutti

No. 27

solo throughout

No. 28

m. 2 solo
m. 83 tutti

m. 128 solo
m. 154 tutti
m. 161 solo
[m. 214 tutti?]
m. 215 tutti
m. 227 solo
m. 269 tutti

No. 30

m. 1 solo
m. 30 tutti
m. 43 solo
m. 122 tutti
m. 137 [solo?]
m. 144 [tutti?]
m. 149 solo
m. 226 tutti
m. 242 solo
m. 248 tutti
m. 253 solo
m. 282 tutti

No. 32

tutti throughout

Appendix 4

Ossia FOR SOLO VOICES IN NO. 19 FROM
Tonkünstler Parts

N.B. The alternative simplified version for the solo voices in No. 19 is given here not because it has any claim to authenticity, but rather because it may prove of use to performers who find the original too difficult.

Appendix 4

Appendix 5

ORIGINAL CONTRABASSOON AND BASS TROMBONE PARTS AS FOUND IN *Tonkünstler, Estate,* AND *Sonnleithner* SETS

CONTRA BASSOON

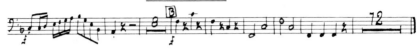

8 RECITATIVE, 9. ARIA TACET

10. RECITATIVE

URIEL

Und die himmlischen Heerscharen ver kün dig ten den dritten Tag. Gott preisend und sprechend:

11. CHORUS

VIVACE

12. RECITATIVE

Zeiten und für Tage und für Jah re Er machte die Sterne gleichfalls

CONTRA BASSOON

PART II
15. RECITATIVE, 16. ARIA, 17. RECITATIVE　Tacet.

18. RECITATIVE
RAPHAEL

Und die Engel rührten ihr'unsterblichen Harfen　und sangen die Wunder und sangen die Wunder des fünften Tag's.

19. TRIO AND CHORUS
MODERATO

20. RECITATIVE RAPHAEL

und Thie.re der Er.de　nach ih _ ren　Gat. tun _ gen.

CONTRA BASSOON

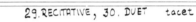

29. RECITATIVE, 30. DUET   tacet

31. RECITATIVE

euch nicht verführt, noch mehr zu wünschen, als ihr habt,   und mehr zu wissen, als ihr sollt!

32. FINAL CHORUS

ANDANTE

ALLEGRO

BASS TROMBONE

5. SOLO WITH CHORUS

ALLEGRO   GABRIEL

des Schöpfers lob, des Schöpfers lob, das lob des zweiten Tags, das lob des zweiten

6. RECITATIVE tacet.

7. ARIA

ALLEGRO ASSAI

14. TRIO AND CHORUS   BASS TROMBONE

jedem Ohre klingend, keiner Zunge fremd, keiner, keiner keiner

Zunge

PART III

27. RECITATIVE

28. DUET WITH CHORUS

BASS TROMBONE

BASS TROMBONE
29. RECITATIVE , 30. DUET tacet

31. RECITATIVE

URIEL.

euch nicht verführt, noch mehr zu wünschen. als ihr habt,   und mehr zu wissen, als ihr sollt!

32. FINAL CHORUS

ANDANTE

BIBLIOGRAPHIC ABBREVIATIONS

N.B. A number of the documents listed below and cited in both the footnotes and Table 1 can be found in translation in Landon/c&w IV–V and Morrow/VIENNA.

AMZ	*Allgemeine Musikalische Zeitung* (Leipzig).
Antonicek/UNIVERSITÄT	Antonicek, Theophil. *Musik im Festsaal der Österreichischen Akademie der Wissenschaften.* Vienna: Böhlaus, 1972.
A-Wgm	Vienna, Gesellschaft der Musikfreunde.
A-Wn	Vienna, Österreichische Nationalbibliothek.
A-Wst	Vienna, Stadtbibliothek.
Barnett/SLURRING	Barnett, Dene. "Non-uniform Slurring in 18th Century Music." *Haydn Yearbook* X (1978): 179–99.
Bartha, Somfai/HOK	Bartha, Dénes, and Somfai, László. *Haydn als Opernkapellmeister. Die Haydn-Documente der Esterházy-Opernsammlung.* Budapest: Verlag der Ungarischen Akademie der Wissenschaften, 1960.
Berwald/ANTECKNINGAR	"Anteckningar utur mitt lif." See Stellan Mörner, "Haydniana aus Schweden um 1800." *Haydn-Studien* II/1 (March 1969): 5–8.
Biba/BEETHOVEN	Biba, Otto. "Beethoven und die 'Liebhaber Concerte' in Wien im Winter 1807–08." *Österreichische Gesellschaft für Musik. Beiträge 76–78. Beethoven-Kolloquium 1977 Documentation und Aufführungspraxis*, pp. 82–93.
Biba/BEISPIELE	Biba, Otto. "Beispiele für die Besetzungsverhältnisse bei Aufführungen von Haydns Oratorien in Wien zwischen 1784 und 1808." *Haydn-Studien* IV/2 (May 1978): 94–104.
Bombet, Gardiner/HAYDN	Bombet, L.A.C. *The Lives of Haydn and Mozart, with Observations on Metastasio, and on the Present State of Music in France and Italy.* Translated from the French of L.A.C. Bombet. With Notes by the Author of the Sacred Melodies [William Gardiner]. 2nd ed. London: Murray, 1818.
Brown/TRAËTTA	Brown, A. Peter. "Tommaso Traëtta and the Genesis of a Haydn Aria (Hob. XXIVb:10)." *Chigiana* XXXVI (1979): 101–42.
Carpani/HAYDINE	Carpani, Giuseppe. *Le Haydine, ovvero lettere su la vita e le opere del celebre maestro Giuseppe Haydn.* Milan: C. Buccinelli, 1812.

Collin/HAYDN'S JUBELFEYER Collin, Heinrich von. "Haydn's Jubelfeyer." *Prometheus* 3 (Vienna: Geistinger, 1808): 87–90.

D-brd-B Berlin, Staatsbibliothek (Stiftung Preussischer Kulturbesitz)

Denkschrift/25 JÄHRIGEN *Denkschrift zur 25 jährigen Jubelfeier der Gesellschaft der Musikfreunde des österreichischen Kaiserstaates durch Aufführung der Schöpfung am. 5 November 1837.* Vienna, 1840.

Deutsch/NELSON & HAYDN Deutsch, Otto Erich. *Admiral Nelson und Haydn. Ein britisch-österreichisches Gipfeltreffen.* Vienna: Österreichischer Bundesverlag, 1982.

Dies/NACHRICHTEN Dies, Albert Christoph. *Biographische Nachrichten von Joseph Haydn.* Vienna. Camesinaische Buchhandlung, 1810. Modern ed. by Horst Seeger. Berlin: Henschelverlag, 1959.

Feder/BEMERKUNGEN Feder, Georg. "Bemerkungen zu Haydns Skizzen." *Beethoven-Jahrbuch* (1973/77): 69–86.

Feder/SKIZZEN Feder, Georg. "Joseph Haydns Skizzen und Entwürfe: Übersicht der Manuscripte, Werkregister, Literatur-und Ausgabenverzeichnis." *Fontes Artis Musicae* XXVI/3 (1979): 172–88.

Geiringer/CREATION Geiringer, Karl. "Haydn's Sketches for 'The Creation.'" *The Musical Quarterly* XVIII/2 (April 1932):299–308.

Griesinger/CORR Correspondence of Georg August Griesinger. Extracts in Edward Olleson, "Georg August Griesinger's Correspondence with Breitkopf & Härtel," *Haydn Yearbook* III (1965): 5–53, and Günter Thomas, "Griesingers Briefe über Haydn. Aus seiner Korrespondenz mit Breitkopf & Härtel," *Haydn-Studien* I/2 (February 1966): 49–114.

Griesinger/NOTIZEN Griesinger, Georg August. *Biographische Notizen über Joseph Haydn.* Leipzig: Breitkopf & Härtel, 1810.

Haydn/BRIEFE *Joseph Haydn: Gesammelte Briefe und Aufzeichnungen.* Ed. Dénes Bartha. Kassel: Bärenreiter, 1965.

HBV "J. Haydns Verzeichniss musikalischer Werke theils eigner, theils fremder Compsition [sic]." British Library, Add. 32070. Known as *Haydn Bibliothek Verzeichnis.*

H-Bn Budapest, Orzágos Széchényi Könyvtár (National Széchényi Library).

Heartz/BURGTHEATER Heartz, Daniel. "Nicholas Jadot and the Building of the Burgtheater." *The Musical Quarterly* LXVIII/1 (January 1982): 1–31.

HMSW-WIGAND

Balthasar Wigand (1770–1846) 51. Sonderausstellung des Historischen Museums der Stadt Wien. 22. September bis 20. November 1977. Vienna: Historischen Museums der Stadt Wien, 1977.

HNV

[*Haydn-Nachlass-Verzeichnis*]. Archiv der Stadt Wien, Personlichkeiten 4/1–4.

Hoboken/HAYDN II

Hoboken, Anthony van. *Joseph Haydn: Thematischbibliographisches Werkverzeichnis. Vol. II: Vokalwerke.* Mainz: B. Schott's Söhne, 1971.

Holschneider/VAN SWIETEN

Holschneider, Andreas. "Die Musikalische Bibliothek Gottfried van Swietens." *Bericht über den Internationalen Musikwissenschaftlichen Kongress, Kassel, 1962.* Ed. Georg Reichert and Martin Just. Kassel: Bärenreiter, 1963, pp. 174–78.

Horn/FIAT LVX

Horn, Hans-Jürgen. "FIAT LVX. Zum Kunsttheoretischen Hintergrund der "Erschaffung' des Lichtes in Haydn's Schöpfung." *Haydn-Studien* III/2 (April 1974): 65–84.

JHW-BH

Joseph Haydn Werke. Leipzig: Breitkopf & Härtel, 1907–33.

JHW-HI

Joseph Haydn Werke. Ed. Joseph Haydn-Institut, Cologne. Munich: G. Henle Verlag, 1958–.

JBTWP

Jahrbuch der Tonkunst von Wien und Prag 1796. Vienna: Schönfeld, 1796. Reprint, ed. Otto Biba. Munich: Katzbichler, 1976.

Jeaffreson/HAMILTON

Jeaffreson, J. *Lady Hamilton and Lord Nelson.* London: 1888. As cited in Landon/C&W IV, p. 560.

Köchel/HK

Köchel, Ludwig Ritter von. *Die Kaiserliche Hof-Musikkapell in Wien von 1543 bis 1867.* Wien: Beck, 1869.

Landon/C&W

Landon, H. C. Robbins. *Haydn: Chronicle and Works.* 5 vols. Bloomington: Indiana University Press, 1976–80.

Larsen, Feder/RICHTLINIEN

Larsen, Jens Peter, and Georg Feder. "Haydn-Ausgabe." In *Editionsrichtlinien musikalischen Denkmäler und Gesamtausgaben.* Ed. Georg von Dadelsen. Kassel: Bärenreiter, 1967, pp. 81–98.

Liechtenstein/CORR

Correspondence of Princess Eleonore von Liechtenstein with her daughter, Countess Josephine von Harrach. Published in Pohl, Botstiber/HAYDN III, pp. 129–31.

Mandyczewski/SCHÖPFUNG

Mandyczewski, Eusebius, ed. *Die Schöpfung. Joseph Haydn Werke* XVI/5. Leipzig: Breitkopf & Härtel, 1922.

Marpurg/KB	Marpurg, F.W. *Kritische Briefe über die Tonkunst.* 3 vols. Berlin: Birnstiel, 1759–64.
MH	*Magyar Hirmondo.*
Morrow/VIENNA	Morrow, Mary Sue. "Concert Life in Vienna, 1776–1810." Ph.D. diss., Indiana University, 1984.
Mosel/UEBERSICHT	Mosel, Ignaz. "Uebersicht des gegenwärtigen Zustandes der Tonkunst in Wien." *Vaterländische Blätter für den österreichischen Kaiserstaat,* Nr. VI/27 (May 1808): 39–44.
Mozart/BRIEFE	Mozart. *Briefe und Aufzeichnungen.* Vol. IV: 1787–1857. Ed. Wilhelm A. Bauer and Otto Erich Deutsch. Kassel: Bärenreiter, 1963.
Müller/DIARIES	Müller, Wenzel. Diaries. Ms. A-Wst. IA 40426, IV 51926.
NTM	*Neue teutsche Merkur.*
Olleson/LIBRETTO	Olleson, D. Edward. "The Origin and Libretto of Haydn's 'Creation.'" *Haydn Yearbook* IV (1968): 148–68.
Osthoff/TROMBE	Osthoff, Wolfgang. "Trombe sordine." *Archiv für Musikwissenschaft* XIII/1 (1956): 77–95.
Plank/DIARIES	Plank, Beda. Diaries. Ms. Stift Kremsmünster. Extracts in Altmann Kellner, *Musikgeschichte des Stiftes Kremsmünster.* Kassel: Bärenreiter, 1956, pp. 541–644.
Pohl/ Botstiber/HAYDN	Pohl, C. F. *Joseph Haydn.* Vol. III (Unter Benutzung der C.F. Pohl hinterlassenen Materialien weitergeführt von Hugo Botstiber). Leipzig: Breitkopf & Härtel, 1927.
Pohl/TKS	Pohl, C. F. *Denkschrift aus Anlass des Hundertjährigen Besthens der Tonkünstler-Societät.* Vienna: Gerold's Sohn, 1871.
PZ	*Pressburger-Zeitung.*
Richter/EIPELDAUER 1799–1800	[Richter, Joseph]. *Der wiederaufgelebte Eipeldauer.* Vienna: Rehm, 1799–1800.
Richter/EIPELDAUER 1802–10	[Richter, Joseph]. *Briefe des junger Eipeldauers an seinen Herrn Vettern in Krakau.* Vienna: Rehm, 1802–10.
Rosenbaum/DIARIES	*The Diaries of Joseph Carl Rosenbaum, 1770–1829.* Extracts ed. Else Radant. *The Haydn Yearbook* V (1968). Complete text in A-Wn Sn. 195–200.
Saslav/TEMPO	Saslav, Isidor. "Tempos in the String Quartets of Joseph Haydn." D.M. document, Indiana University, 1969.

Schmid/ZIERPRAXIS   Schmid, Ernst Fritz. "Joseph Haydn und die vokale Zierpraxis seiner Zeit, dargestellt an einer Arie seines Tobias-Oratoriums." *Bericht über die Internationale Konferenz zum Andenken Joseph Haydns. Budapest 17.–22. September 1959.* Ed. Bence Szabolcsi and Dénes Bartha. Budapest: Akadémiai Kiadó, 1961.

Seyfried/DIARIES   Seyfried, Ignaz Ritter von. Diaries. Ms. A-Wst. IB 84958.

Silverstolpe/REPORTS   Silverstolpe, F. S. [Reports] in C. G. Stellan Mörner, "Haydniana aus Schweden." *Haydn-Studien* II/1 (March 1969): 25–26.

Smiles/ORNAMENTATION   Smiles, Joan E. "Improvised Ornamentation in Late Eighteenth-Century Music: An Examination of Contemporary Evidence." Ph.D. diss., Stanford University, 1975.

Södermanland/DIARIES   Södermanland, Duchess Hedvig Charlotta. Diaries. Extracts published in C. G. Stellan Mörner, *Johan Wikmanson und die Brüder Silverstolpe.* Uppsala: Almquist & Wiksell, 1952, pp. 334–40.

Stern/SCHÖPFUNG   Stern, Martin. "Haydns 'Schöpfung.' Geist und Herkunft des van Swietenschen Librettos. Ein Beitrag zum Thema 'Sakularisation' im Zeitalter der Aufklarung." *Haydn-Studien* I/3 (October 1966): 121–98.

Temperley/ENGLISH   Temperley, Nicholas. "New Light on the Libretto of *The Creation.*" *Music in Eighteenth-Century England. Essays in Memory of Charles Cudworth.* Ed. Christopher Hogwood and Richard Luckett. Cambridge: Cambridge University Press, 1983.

TK   Tonkünstler-Societät Performing Materials

Turgenev/CORR   Turgenev, Alexander Ivanovitsch. Correspondence as quoted in Boris Steinpress, "Haydns Oratorien in Russland. Zu Lebzeiten des Komponisten." *Haydn-Studien* II/2 (May 1969): 91–92.

Walter/SCHÖPFUNG   Walter, Horst. "Gottfried van Swietens handschriftliche Textbücher zu 'Schöpfung' und 'Jahreszeiten.' " *Haydn-Studien* I/4 (April 1967): 241–77.

Wolff/ISHAM III   Wolff, Christoph, ed. *The String Quartets of Haydn, Mozart, and Beethoven: Studies of the Autograph Manuscripts. A Conference at Isham Memorial Library March 15–17, 1979.* Cambridge: Harvard, 1980.

WTA   *Wiener Theater Almanach.*

WTZ   *Wiener Theater Zeitung* (1806?–1808).

WZ   *Wiener-Zeitung.*

Zaslaw/REVIVAL Zaslaw, Neal. "Toward the Revival of the Classical Orchestra." *Proceedings of the Royal Musical Association* CIII (1976–77): 158–87.

Zeman/SCHÖPFUNG Zeman, Herbert. "Das Textbuch Gottfried van Swietens zu Joseph Haydns 'Die Schöpfung.' " *Die Österreichische Literature ihr Profil an der Wende vom 18. zum 19. Jahrhundert (1750–1830)*. Ed. Herbert Zeman. Graz: Akademische Druck- und Verlagsanstalt, 1979, pp. 403–26.

Zinzendorf/DIARIES Zinzendorf, Count Karl von. "Diaries." Haus- Hof- und Staatsarchiv, Vienna.

NOTES

1. Sources

1. For *The Creation*, the recent literature has been chiefly concerned with the libretto. Among the most important contributions have been: Olleson/LIBRETTO, Stern/SCHÖPFUNG, Temperley/ENGLISH, Waltcr/SCHÖPFUNG, and Zeman/SCHÖPFUNG.

2. Mandyczewski/SCHÖPFUNG. To cite but two errors in the edition: no. 9, m. 81, last three notes in soprano should read B-flat, C, A (see Ex. 19); no. 24, the cello and bass parts should read C-natural (m. 37), C-sharp (m. 38), D (m. 39).

3. On the sketches, see Feder/BEMERKUNGEN, Feder/SKIZZEN, Geiringer/CREATION, and Landon/C&W IV, pp. 352–88.

4. See Griesinger/CORR, 3 July 1801, Dies/NACHRICHTEN, p. 182, and Holschneider/VAN SWIETEN.

5. Copyist numbers derive from Bartha, Somfai/HOK, p. 423.

6. According to Walter/SCHÖPFUNG, p. 249, Landon/C&W IV, p. 392, and Temperley/ENGLISH, p. 194.

7. Landon/C&W IV, p. 392.

8. Hoboken/HAYDN II, p. 36.

9. "Noch Eins: Wie ich geshehen besitz d. Haydn-Verein die Orchesterstimmen zur Schöpfung, geschreiben von Elssler mit zahlreichen Bemerkungen versehen vom Haydn's Hand! Diese Hefte waren seit 1799 in gebrauch. Und niemand ahndte welcher Schatz der Verein da besitzt." Brahms *Nachlass*, A-Wgm. My thanks to Dr. Otto Biba for bringing this letter to my attention and allowing me to quote from it.

10. Landon/C&W IV, p. 391.

11. A list of the performers is given in Biba/BEETHOVEN, p. 87, but to this must be added one flute, contrabassoon, and three trombones.

12. My thanks to Dr. Otto Biba for bringing these incompletely catalogued parts to my attention.

13. Landon/C&W IV, pp. 391–92.

2. Forces, Scoring, and Dynamics

1. AMZ 1799, No. 21 (20 February), col. 335.

2. Mozart/BRIEFE, p. 232.

3. AMZ 1799, No. 28 (10 April), cols. 445–46 (footnote).

4. Berwald/ANTECKNINGAR.

5. *Der Sammler* (21 April 1810). See Table 1, no. 45.

6. A conclusion reached from the lists of members in Pohl/TKS, pp. 103–27.

7. See Biba/BEISPIELE.

8. See Biba/BEISPIELE and Köchel/HK.

9. Plank/DIARIES, 16 January 1801, and Pohl/TKS, p. 51. See also Mosel/UEBERSICHT, p. 41.

10. See Denkschrift/25 JÄHRIGEN.

11. Carpani/HAYDINE, p. 186.

12. Turgenev/CORR.

13. AMZ 1810, No. 14 (3 January), col. 219.

14. Biba/BEISPIELE, p. 100.

15. Denkschrift/25 JÄHRIGEN.

16. Bombet, Gardiner/HAYDN, p. 230.

17. Reprinted in Landon/C&W V, pp. 132–37.

18. Haydn/BRIEFE, pp. 58–60.

19. Bombet, Gardiner/HAYDN, p. 231. Gardiner continues with one of the most imaginative solutions to the problem of the weak bass:

> The instruments at present known, are inadequate to pour upon the orchestra that volume of sound, which the pieces of the great German composers demand. It is in the lower regions of the scale, that we are most deficient in power. One or two octaves have been added to its height, during the last century, but no one has yet dared the "unfathomable depths" of harmony. The magnitude of sound desired, might perhaps be obtained by causing large bodies to revolve in the air by means of machinery. The note produced would depend on their form, and the degree of rapidity with which they were whirled. Immense tubes upon the principle of the *trombone* might also be worked by the same means, so as to descend two octaves below that instrument. It is only by means of engines of this kind, that the grand orchestra can be brought to perfection, or the full effect of many awful combinations of the modern art displayed.

20. For the other surviving sets of parts, all presumably used for less ambitious renditions, such a distinction does not exist, as the continuo part was seemingly played from the first desks within the orchestral group.

21. Berwald/ANTECKNINGAR.

22. See also Zaslaw/REVIVAL, p. 165, also in *The New Grove* XIII, p. 684, and Biba/BEISPIELE.

23. A similar placement of forces is described in Marpurg/KB I (19 April 1760), p. 347:

> Der Ort, wo das Oratorium vorgestellet werden sollte, war ein sehr geraumer und schön erleuchteter Schauplatz. Die ganze Musik befand sich auf dem Theater. Vorn an sassen die Sänger, und hinter ihnen die Instrumentisten, in guter Ordnung, auf immer hinter einander stufenweise erhöhten Banken. In der Mitte dieses Amphitheaters stand ein Positiv, welches aber beynahe die Grosse einer kleinen Orgel hatte. Auf diesen wurden, wie ich in der Folge bemerkte, nur die Tutti und Ritornellé mit accompagniret. Bey dem Solosatzen und den Recitativen aber, wurde der Generalbass auf zween starken und heilklingenden Flügeln gespielt.

> The place where the oratorio was supposed to be presented was a very roomy, beautifully lit arena. All the performers were on the stage. The singers sat in front; behind them (were) the instrumentalists, well arranged on benches raised stepwise behind each other. In the middle of this amphitheater was a Positif, which was, however, almost as large as a small organ. As I subsequently noticed, only the tuttis and ritornellos were accompanied on it. In the solo movements and recitatives the continuo was played on two powerful, robust-sounding harpsichords.

See also Heartz/BURGTHEATER, pp. 23–25.

24. See the discussion on this point by Larsen and Biba at the end of Biba/BEETHOVEN, pp. 92–93. The best summaries of the extensive literature for this occasion are found in Antonicek/UNIVERSITÄT, pp. 35–41, and Landon/C&W V, pp. 358–64.

25. See literature for performance no. 40, Table 1.
26. See HMSW-WIGAND for an overview of his work.
27. Landon/C&W IV, p. 395.
28. See Osthoff/TROMBE. The mournful association of muted trumpets and timpani was also current in Vienna: the Albertina owns a watercolor from 1770, *Ein Leichenbegängnis 1770*, in which the trumpets and drums participating are muted (Vienna: Graphische Sammlung Albertina, Historische Blätter Wien III, 1750–1782, Blaue Nr. 32). See *Joseph Haydn in seiner Zeit, Eisenstadt, 20. Mai-26. Oktober 1982*. (Exhibition Catalogue). Eisenstadt 1982, No. 517. Haydn's only other employment of mutes for the brass and drums is in the slow movement of Symphony No. 102.
29. "Da prima voi sentite un sommesso ed indeciso sorgere di tuoni . . . ", Carpani/HAYDINE, p. 172.
30. See Silverstolpe/REPORTS. The whole aesthetic background to this gesture is found in Horn/FIAT LVX.
31. See the discussion in Wolff/ISHAM III, pp. 5–120 passim.
32. William Gardiner again contributes a fanciful explication of this passage based on the reading of the first edition:

Perhaps there is nothing in nature, which is capable of being so well represented, by sound, as light. The answer of the blind man, who, on being asked what idea he had of scarlet, replied, that it was like the sound of a trumpet, is less absurd than may at first be apprehended. It should be observed, that the character of different instruments depends not merely on the acuteness or gravity of their tone, but, also, on the degree of force with which sounds are produced by them. If, as Sir Isaac Newton supposed, the impulse upon the nerves of the eye, produced by colours, is similar in kind or degree to that produced upon the ear by sounds, the impression upon the sensorium, or seat of sensation in the brain, will probably be the same, or so nearly so, that the ideas of the respective external objects will be associated in the mind. According to this theory, the different musical instruments may be characterized by corresponding colours, so as to be fancifully classed in the following manner: Wind Instruments: Trombone–Deep Red, Trumpet–Scarlet, Clarionette [*sic*]–Orange, Oboe–Yellow, Bassoon (Alto)–Deep Yellow, Flute–Sky Blue, Diapason–Deeper Blue, Double Diapason–Purple, Horn–Violet; Stringed Instruments: Violin–Pink, Viola–Rose, Violoncello–Red, Double bass–Deep crimson red.
    The sinfonia in *The Creation*, which represents the rising of the sun, is an exemplification of this theory. In the commencement of this piece, our attention is attracted by a soft streaming note from the violins, which is scarcely discernible, till the rays of sound which issue from the second violin, diverge into the chord of the second, to which is gradually imparted a greater fulness of colour as the violas and violoncellos steal in with expanding harmony.
    At the fifth bar, the oboes begin to shed their yellow lustre, while the flute silvers the mounting rays of the violin. As the notes continue ascending to the highest point of brightness, the orange, the scarlet, and the purple, unite in the increasing splendour; and the glorious orb at length appears refulgent with all the brightest beams of harmony.

Bombet, Gardiner/HAYDN, pp. 255–56.
33. Walter/SCHÖPFUNG, pp. 253–54; Landon/C&W IV, p. 351.

3. Embellishment and Ornamentation

1. Bartha, Somfai/HOK, p. 57.
2. Published in JHW-HI XXVIII/1/1 and in Schmid/ZIERPRAXIS.

3. "Questa musica va eseguita con semplicità, esattezza, espressione e por-
tamento, ma senza *fiorettare*." Carpani/HAYDINE, p. 182.

4. Dies/NACHRICHTEN, p. 167. There are two other tangential statements
from the same period. The first concerns an unidentified Haydn Mass. One
Herr Schmith wrote to the Philharmonic Society in Laibach that Haydn performed his mass without "unnecessary ornamentation, which is of no use except to damage such a most delicate composition since [it] already contains all
sorts of expression" (Landon/C&W IV, pp. 567–68). The second refers to
Therese Saal, who sang the solo soprano more than a dozen times, many of
them under Haydn's direction. According to the *Zeitung für elegante Welt*
1803, No. 76, her "simple, sincere and appropriate delivery show more feeling
for art and more correct judgement than all of the runs and embellishments so
often and inappropriately interpolated . . ." (Landon/C&W V, p. 37).

5. See, for example, Haydn's more modest fermata elaboration from the
mid-1780s in the sketch to his tenor insertion aria for Traëtta's *Ifigenia in
Tauride.* See Brown/TRAËTTA, p. 120.

6. For a sampling of theoretical opinions, see Smiles/ORNAMENTATION, pp.
180–81, 188, 253, 258, 289, 339, 343, 350, and 420.

4. Bowing and Articulation

1. Dies/NACHRICHTEN, pp. 84–85. See also Landon's gloss on this passage
in C&W III, pp. 54–55.

2. For the best treatments of this problem, see Larsen, Feder/RICHTLINIEN,
p. 93, and Wolff/ISHAM III, pp. 5–120 passim. See also the controversial study,
Barnett/SLURRING.

3. Landon/C&W IV, pp. 396–97.

5. Tempo

1. Haydn/BRIEFE, pp. 58–60.
2. Completely documented in Bartha, Somfai/HOK.
3. Haydn/BRIEFE, pp. 388–89.
4. Plank/DIARIES, pp. 567–68.
5. Griesinger/CORR, 21 January 1801.

6. Conclusion

1. Griesinger/CORR, 26 December 1801. See *Haydn-Studien* I/2 (February
1966): 82.

2. AMZ, *Intelligenz Blatt* XV (June 1799), cols. 73–74, as trans. in
Landon/C&W IV, p. 471.

3. Dies/NACHRICHTEN, pp. 158–59; Griesinger/NOTIZEN, p.37.

4. *The Times* and *Morning Chronicle,* 27 March 1800; *Morning Herald,*
29 March 1800, as quoted from Landon/C&W IV, p. 573.

5. *The Times,* 1 April 1800; *Morning Chronicle,* 31 March 1800; *Morning
Herald,* 2 April 1800, as quoted from Landon/C&W IV, p. 575.

6. *The Times,* 4 April 1800, as quoted from Landon/C&W IV, p. 575.

INDEX

THE CREATION, NUMBERS CITED